People as Care Catalysts

People as Care Catalysts

From being patient to becoming healthy

Edited by Richard Normann and Niklas Arvidsson

John Wiley & Sons, Ltd

Other Wiley Editorial Offices

John Wiley & Sons Inc., 111 River Street, Hoboken, NJ 07030, USA

Jossey-Bass, 989 Market Street, San Francisco, CA 94103-1741, USA

Wiley-VCH Verlag GmbH, Boschstr. 12, D-69469 Weinheim, Germany

John Wiley & Sons Australia Ltd, 42 McDougall Street, Milton, Queensland 4064, Australia

John Wiley & Sons (Asia) Pte Ltd, 2 Clementi Loop #02-01, Jin Xing Distripark, Singapore
129809

John Wiley & Sons Canada Ltd, 22 Worcester Road, Etobicoke, Ontario, Canada M9W 1L1

Wiley also publishes its books in a variety of electronic formats. Some content that appears in
print may not be available in electronic books.

Library of Congress Cataloging-in-Publication Data

People as care catalysts : from being patient to becoming healthy /
    [edited] by Richard Normann and Niklas Arvidsson. — 1st ed.
      p.   cm.
    ISBN 13 978-0-470-01778-4
    ISBN 10 0-470-01778-3
    1. Medical care—Europe.   2. Medical policy—Europe.
  3. Patients—Services for—Europe.   4. Patients—Europe—Attitudes.
  I. Normann, Richard, 1943–   . II. Arvidsson, Niklas.
    [DNLM: 1. Delivery of Health Care—Europe.   2. Health
  Policy—Europe.   3. Patients—Europe.   4. Attitude to Health—Europe.
  W 84 GA1 P419 2006]
  RA395.E85P45 2006
  362.1094—dc22   2005026873

British Library Cataloguing in Publication Data

A catalogue record for this book is available from the British Library

ISBN 13 978-0-470-01778-4 (HB)
ISBN 10 0-470-01778-3 (HB)

Typeset in 11/16pt Trump Medieval by SNP Best-set Typesetter Ltd., Hong Kong
Printed and bound in Great Britain by TJ International Ltd., Padstow, Cornwall, UK
This book is printed on acid-free paper responsibly manufactured from sustainable forestry in
which at least two trees are planted for each one used for paper production.

Contents

List of contributors

Richard Normann

(1943–2003) Professor. Founder of NormannPartners and Service Management Group (SMG). A leading strategy and management thinker and international advisor. Major contributions on how to radically rethink business, create value and sustain excellence, and author of numerous books such as *Reframing Business*, *Service Management* and *Designing Interactive Strategy*.

Niklas Arvidsson

Researcher at National Institute of Working Life, Sweden; PhD International Business; former colleague of Richard Normann at SMG.

National Institute for Working Life, SE-113 91 Stockholm, Sweden. Email niklas.arvidsson@arbetslivsinstitutet.se

Gordon Best

Founding Director, ODN Partnerships Network.

OD Partnerships Network, 55 St John Street, London EC1M 4AN, United Kingdom. Email gordonbest@odpn.co.uk

Christophe Courbage

PhD Economics; The Geneva Association.

Geneva Association – Health and Ageing Research Program, Route de Malagnou, 53, CH-1208 Geneva, Switzerland. Email christophe_courbage@genevaassociation.org

Michel Crozier

Membre de l'Institut; Professor emeritus de sociologie IEP de Paris.

116 Avenue Général Leclerc, Paris 14, France.

Orio Giarini

Professor; Director, The Risk Institute, Geneva-Trieste.

10 via della Torretta, 34121 Trieste, ITALY. Email orio.giarini@alice.it

John Harries

Associate, OD Partnerships Network.

BT, Level 6, 1 Drury Lane, Covent Garden, London WC2B 5RS, United Kingdom. Email john.harries@bcs.org

Bert Levin

Master of Law; former Under-secretary of State; former colleague of Richard Normann at SMG.

Malmgårdsvägen 6, SE-11638 Stockholm, Sweden. Email bert.levin@wanadoo.fr

Michael Maccoby

President of The Maccoby Group; Director of the Project on Technology, Work and Character (a not for profit organization); From 1978–90 Director of the Program on Technology, Public Policy and Human Development at Harvard.

The Maccoby Group, 4825 Linnean Avenue, NW, Washington, DC 20008, USA. Email mm@maccoby.com

Foreword

IN NOVEMBER 2003 THE INTERNATIONAL COMMUNITY LOST ONE of its most valuable citizens. Richard Normann's battle with cancer ended after a valiant and tenacious effort to fight the spread of the disease throughout his body. True to his principles, and to the title of this book, he was coproducing his health care to the very end.

Likewise, the consulting, writing and collaborating that defined his life filled those days with purpose. With limited time, but an infinite number of opportunities to apply his prodigious intellect, he chose to focus his last years on health and health care, with specific application to the European social welfare states. He was attracted to the entrepreneurial characteristics of the US health care system, but disturbed by the fragmentation and lack of social justice that he perceived in the result. His interest was captured by non-traditional approaches in US organizations such as United-Healthcare and the Premier, Inc. healthcare alliance.

Ultimately, however, he reflected primarily on the strengths (and weaknesses) of the French and Swedish health systems. One result of his broad perspective across nations is that his ideas for designing new health systems are relevant around the globe.

By seeing this book through to completion, Niklas Arvidsson, PhD, has helped further the contribution of Richard and collaborators, intelligently assembling content and commentary to provide clarity of main themes. And to engage readers intellectually as well – there is no superficiality here.

I was introduced to Richard in 1998 by Gordon Best and was immediately attracted by his unique ability to organize complex concepts into elegantly simple frameworks that appeared on chart pads or on his aging collection of overhead transparencies. In turn, Richard was intrigued by the potential of an alliance such as Premier to fundamentally improve the performance of the US health care system.

Reflecting learning captured in this book, for example, it is clear that improving the cost and quality performance of episodes of acute care in US hospitals has been necessary, but not sufficient, for meaningful system improvement. Indeed, to focus primarily on acute hospital care would relegate these organizations to the role of 'high-tech manufacturing plants', with customers being aggregated by the aggressive and innovative tactics of UnitedHealthcare and others. Improved performance means that systems of care must be built to serve populations with common health needs. Deep knowledge of customers and even 'customers' customers' is a prerequisite.

Engaging customers in the 'coproduction' of their health care needs provides needed resources, integration of care, loyalty and the opportunity to build care communities. Value for customers involves engaging them meaningfully in the production of their care and not just in the consumption of professionally produced health services.

Organizations that can display 'prime movership' in building 'value constellations' (networks) can be the catalysts for needed systemic change. Technology can provide the opportunity for these networks to be freed from space, time and geographic constraints, while delighting customers. These concepts have guided the strategy development for Premier and irrevocably changed the perspective that I bring to health care.

In this book, contributions by Richard and his collaborators build to the idea of an idealized design of the health care system. The basic conclusions of 'fairness/solidarity/risk-sharing, quality and rationality' provide the solid foundation for the implementation of his ideas. Ultimately, the positive economic characteristics of health, including productivity, creativity and longevity, with wisdom, suggest that the efficient and effective operation of health systems can be a true asset to society instead of a perceived cost burden.

This is the health care system legacy of Richard Normann. His legacy for those of us who knew him and worked with him is an indomitable spirit that drove him to research his disease, partake in advanced clinical research, self-medicate and remain productive and active to the end. Coupled with his love of good food, wine and companionship, and livened with his dry sense of humor, it is quite a legacy!

Richard A. Norling, President and Chief Executive Officer,
Premier, Inc., San Diego, California, USA
June 16th, 2005

Preface – how this book came about

FOR A LONG TIME, HEALTH CARE AND OLD-AGE CARE HAVE been regarded as central parts of the politically organized welfare system. In Europe, this has resulted in a high degree of tax financing, a high degree of public ownership of production resources and in the end has resulted in a political responsibility for welfare. The European systems tend to be essentially monolithic while the US system is fragmented, in spite of efforts to introduce 'managed care'.

There are two central elements of health care systems (see Figure 1.1). There is an axis from health promotion to care of the sick and elderly, another axis from public to private. Already, this simple matrix illustrates the mixture of the financing of the health system. Tax financing, private insurance, direct payments by the individuals and employer financing all exist in different combinations. There is a pattern of heavier tax financing – but not at all exclusively – regarding care of the ill compared to health promotion, and inversely different forms of private financing dominate the health promotion area. This pattern is seen in many systems of the most economically developed countries.

There is an emerging trend in which financing and production of services within the health care system have been separated. The quest for more efficiency and cost reduction sometimes results in different types of market solution. Later, we will come back with critical reflections on some elements of this development. Internationally, this development is obvious, but we also see it in bastions of public control of production, such as the UK and Sweden.

Health care is, by many measures, one of the fastest growing areas of activity in the world. Many different actors, including institutional actors and business organizations, are involved in health care. These include companies whose core competence is in health care – e.g. pharmaceutical companies, care-producing companies and medical technology companies – but also companies in other industries but with key applications within the care area, like information and communication technology. Together these forces are gradually coming to challenge the way health care systems are shaped.

Several stories meet in this book – like ships meeting at sea. No doubt many of these ships will continue on their respective journeys rather than forming an armada. But the meeting was not just a coincidence and each ship will hopefully bear the marks of the meeting as it carries on. I will tell the story of this meeting from my own vantage point.

With a professional background in the interdisciplinary field of organization theory, I have always been fascinated by health care. My encounters with it were sporadic for a long time, both in my role as a researcher and as a consultant. As our family emigrated from Sweden (with its – self imposed? – reputation as one of the best, if not the best, health care system in the world) to France in 1977, it came almost as a physical shock to find that we actually had access to physicians and freedom to choose between them. The health care system was there, it was not beyond reach. For me, the French system was so much better than the Swedish one that there was almost no comparison.

In my sphere as a professional I first looked at a couple of cases of pharmaceutical companies as part of my studies of innovativeness for my doctoral thesis. This was around 1970. I then had the opportunity to work with the Danish Pharmacists' Association on a broad 'perspective plan' in the early and mid 1980s (summarized in Normann and Ramirez, 1993). This gave me an insight into how regulations and politics could effectively create inefficiency and imprison knowledge that could have been used to much better advantage. I am still deeply in dept to Peter Kielgast, then General Secretary of the Danish Pharmacists' Association, for his insight, foresight and continuing battle on a global scale as he later on became president of FIP, Féderation Internationale Pharmaceutique.

It was only, however, in the late 1990s that I got the opportunity to pull various pieces together and look at health care in a more integrated way. Perhaps it was the emergence of a slightly changed climate in Sweden, where some sacred cows now seemed less imperturbable. Perhaps it was extra motivation from the fact that my wife had gone through – successfully – breast cancer treatment at home in France, and that I myself had been diagnosed with a carcinoid in an advanced stage – so I had had ample opportunity to get not only the researcher's and consultant's, but also the citizen's and the patient's and the human being's perspective. In any case, with support from my colleague Bert Levin, we were able to initiate and stage a major, overriding project in the southern region of Sweden. This project was unique in that it gathered an extremely broad constituency of stakeholders and competencies, and in that it was both analytical and design oriented. It was summarized in a book in Swedish (Levin and Normann, 2000). That book has provided certain contributions to the present book. My personal insights into health care continue to be deepened by – among other activities – an ongoing major project in the United States.

All the other contributions have been written specifically for this book. While – like the Swedish study – they come out of different national perspectives (USA, UK, France and Switzerland) their scope is not national but much broader (Chapter 5, while focusing on the evolution of the French health care system, tells us a great deal about the more general evolution of the European welfare state paradigm). They all deepen and complement the argument. They are all written by people with whom I share an intellectual affinity and with most of whom I have had a long working relationship. I contacted and encouraged each of the authors to make a contribution in the area that will interest them the most and which would complement the work we had done on the Swedish system, which they got the opportunity to read before they wrote their chapters.

Michel Crozier's chapter (Chapter 5) has a broad scope and looks at the architecture of the whole system, but it adds a deep historical perspective. The French system came together after the Second World War, but gradually has become increasingly institutionalized and entrenched and therefore unable to alter itself. The stakes of the various actors originally involved were once well balanced, but now work in directions that make it difficult to adapt to the new technological and demographic challenges. Moreover, citizens have learned to take advantage of the system, and practitioners and citizens tend to collude against change. Politicians, particularly leftist ones, suspicious of a two-track system, try to contain cost but prevent structural change.

Michel Crozier calls for broad reforms in three directions, all in consonance with the principles of the 'idealized design' of the Swedish study (Levin and Normann, 2000): a reinterpretation for today's new situation of the principle of equality of access; public health; and – using very powerful language – 'a new regulation that liberates the State from its impossible responsibility'.

I find the last direction particularly striking since it corresponds so well with the conclusion on the role of politicians from the Swedish study: as long as politicians put themselves in the position of being 'factory managers', they will diminish their power to be effective regulators, and therefore their very attempt to cling to their power will make them increasingly powerless.

Chapter 6 deepens the analysis in two areas: demographics as a driving force making change necessary and inevitable, and the consequences for financing of post retirement and health care. The new risk panorama cannot be handled by 'pay-as-you-go' systems. The analysis in this chapter goes a long way to laying bare the different underlying risks and the different cost drivers, to indicating differentiated means of financing and managing risks, and to shifting the risk management burden to the respective actors with the appropriate means and motivations for each type of risk. In fact, Courbage and Giarini provide a framework to answer many of the challenges posed by Crozier. In doing this they point in directions which are inevitable but which – as is also Crozier's message – transcend the simplistic solutions and traditional myths still tending to guide politicians.

Chapter 4, in different ways, illustrates related themes. There are interesting indications here about how to design coproductive systems that avoid the collusion of actors to rob the system that pay-as-you-go schemes tend to create, or the crude and unfair rationing models that politicians and governments seem to favour when they are unable to develop more creative ideas.

Best and Harries have chosen to use a specific, but hopefully important, framework from my publications (Normann, 2000a, 2000b; Normann and Ramirez, 1994) for an intellectual exercise with practical illustrations. This approach and this framework were also important in the Swedish study, but Best and Harries take it further into concrete implications. They aim to explore how a system could be designed in which a more coproductive relationship between the citizen/customer/patient (to use an expression elaborated in the Swedish study) and the provider system could be developed, and in what situations this would be appropriate. They use my concepts of 'enabling' and 'relieving' to indicate different ways in which activities and functions could be transferred from the system to patients in order to increase efficiency and quality. Like the Swedish study, their analysis also indicates to what a great extent the current system is characterized by a 'relieving' mode, in which the patient is seen as a passive and unknowing receiver of services provided by experts in a service factory. This view is based on a model of health care moulded in the tradition of industrial production.

And this brings us to the chapter by Michael Maccoby (Chapter 7). His report from a research project involving several clinics in the USA tracks health care in an anthropological perspective and in terms of the historical transition from health care as a craft-based cottage industry via health care as an industrialized bureaucracy ('McMedicine' focused factory) towards an alternative model. He frames the current situation as a transition of society into an 'age of learning', which requires a new leadership model that takes into account both variability and efficiency, and where coproduction and creativity, as well as health and patient orientation, are cornerstones.

The application of such a model would, in addition to increasing quality, efficiency and value, ultimately lead to a system with a higher capacity of enabling, including self-enabling. This would go a long way to answering a common call from all of the contributions to this book: a system with much higher self-organizing capacity. To achieve such capacity we must, first of all, recognize that the complexity of health care is much, much too high for anybody to design it top down or to try to apply any kind of traditional philosophy of management by control. Secondly, a charter must be defined in which each and every one of the actors are activated, enabled and entrusted with making the contributions and priorities appropriate to that actor.

I hope the reader will see and appreciate the strong unity in the diversity of perspectives offered by this book.

Richard Normann

Acknowledgements

MICHAEL MACCOBY EXPRESSES GRATITUDE TO THE Robert Wood Johnson Foundation for funding his research. He was assisted by Richard Margolies, Barbara Lenkerd and Doug Wilson, and is grateful for counsel from an advisory committee including: Polly Bdnash, PhD, RN, FAAN, Executive Director, American Association of Colleges of Nursing; Roger Bulger, MD, President, Association of Academic Health Centers; Paul Griner, MD, former President, American College of Physicians and Vice President and Director, Center for the Assessment and Management of Change in Academic Medicine, Association of American Medical Colleges; Federico Ortiz Quesada, MD, formerly Director, International Relations, Mexican Ministry of Health; Stan Pappelbaum, MD, former CEO, Scripps Health; Richard Riegelman, MD, MPH, PhD, formerly Dean, School of Public Health and Health Services, George Washington University; and Henry Simmons, MD, President, National Leadership Coalition on Health Care.

We want to acknowledge Bertil and Marie Ekerlid at Ekerlids Förlag, who published the embryo to this book, namely *Vårdens Chans*, and who supported our ambitions to publish this book.

We are also indebted to Ulf Mannervik and NormannPartners AB who have supported this project from the start and provided helpful thoughts and support all the way to the final manuscript.

1

Challenges for health care in Western societies

Richard Normann

'We have to change in order to stay the same'

Could it be that public health care systems in Europe are digging their own graves by not reinterpreting their identity and design sufficiently in a new situation and by too single-handedly sticking to principles that served in the past but will now cause them to lose control?

Health care is regarded as a central part of welfare systems. In Europe, this has resulted in a high degree of tax financing, a high degree of public ownership of production resources and in political responsibility for welfare. The European systems tend to be essentially monolithic while the US system is fragmented, in spite of efforts to introduce 'managed care'.

People as Care Catalysts: From being patient to becoming healthy. Edited by R. Normann and N. Arvidsson. © 2006 John Wiley & Sons, Ltd.

A schematic matrix (see Figure 1.1) can illustrate the central elements of health care systems. One axis ranges from health and wellbeing promotion to care of the sick and elderly, another axis distinguishes financing from public to private. (Financing and production are not logically linked, but in practice, European health care systems have mixed the two and the overwhelming bulk of care production is not only publicly financed but also publicly produced.) Tax financing, private insurance, direct payments by the individuals and employer financing, however, exist in different combinations.

The quest for higher efficiency and cost reduction sometimes results in different types of market solution, even in bastions of public financing and production such as the UK and Sweden.

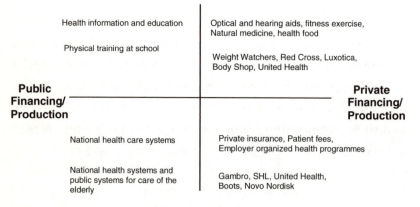

Promotion of health

Health information and education

Physical training at school

Optical and hearing aids, fitness exercise, Natural medicine, health food

Weight Watchers, Red Cross, Luxotica, Body Shop, United Health

Public Financing/ Production

Private Financing/ Production

National health care systems

National health systems and public systems for care of the elderly

Private insurance, Patient fees, Employer organized health programmes

Gambro, SHL, United Health, Boots, Novo Nordisk

Care of the ill and elderly

Figure 1.1 Central elements in health care systems.

Health care is, by any measure, one of the fastest growing domains of activity in the world. With dramatic (but entirely foreseeable) demographic changes under way, with the advent of the informed citizen/customer/patient, and with scientific and technological developments that will sooner or later create a range of breakthroughs, this trend can only be reinforced. A great diversity of institutional actors and business organizations are involved in care-related activities. The latter include companies whose core competence is in health care – e.g. pharmaceutical companies, care-producing companies and medical technology companies – but also industries with central applications within areas like information and communication technology. Together these forces are gradually coming to reshape the way health systems in many countries are functioning.

Two alternatives for public health systems

It is the lower left square of our matrix that is referred to most frequently when we talk about public health systems. It represents *treatment of manifest illness* and is based on *public financing*. WHO, however, in recent reports and plans emphasizes the importance of the 'stewardship' of politics covering the whole system, implying a perspective on all four squares.

Let us make a few comments on the other three squares of Figure 1.1. The *publicly financed system concentrated on health* is also well known in Europe. The work done by public health bodies and sports and gymnastics at school are good examples of this kind of focusing. However, today there are indications in several countries that activities in this domain are being sacrificed on the altar of budgetary restrictions.

Health and *'other' financing* appear to be in a state of strong expansion. Here we find investments in functional foods, some natural medicines, lifestyle medicines and alternative treatments, strong health orientation in the media, etc. The pharmaceutical industry is increasing its activity in this area, not only concerning spectacular products like Viagra, but also by trying systematically to reach 'end consumers' via various media, including the Internet and through OTC products. Examples are known in which companies like Weight Watchers even have a hard time taking care of the onrush of customers. Many new kinds of companies and institutions can be expected to appear in this square. In a study by The Institute for the Future, it is predicted that health care will be the very engine of economic growth in the near future, and that health considerations will comprise not only traditional health care, but pervade a range of other industries as well. Indeed, they see us entering 'the health care economy'.

Finally, the sector *'other financing/illness'* is also undergoing strong expansion. An increasing number of people – notably knowledge workers and their employers – are heavily dependent on immediate access to diagnosis and therapy and will therefore look for different forms of care. Several insurance companies have developed specific solutions combined with contracted care suppliers, including non-domestic ones. New care alternatives will arise for people, both inside and outside their home country and on both a small and a large scale.

On the right – non-public financing – side of our matrix, we also find a strong increase in personal life and savings products that increase preparedness for facing the future and old age. Many driving forces are behind this development. Displeasure with the unavailability and often long waiting times of the established system has resulted in unacceptable situations for many people. Internationalization and globalization create new openings. At the same time there is of course discontent – not yet very organized – due to the fact that you may be charged twice for your care.

There are also strong indications of *preparedness to pay more for one's health*. Ever more people realize that health is not only the absence of illness. Business companies understand that an increased supply of health-creating and lifestyle-improving offerings also creates demand. (Perhaps politicians and those responsible for public health systems also realize this, but they tend to see it as a major problem.) It is conceivable that in some countries as much as a doubling of health related spending (as part of per capita GNP) may occur in the not too distant future. Since the public system today already has a hard time fulfilling what people consider its task, and at the same time is concentrated on cost reduction, the growth on 'the right side' may become very strong, almost explosive. Taking this as a point of departure, you can see two scenario alternatives today.

In the *first scenario alternative*, publicly financed care continues to focus on cost cutting and is unable to introduce a creative and adaptive organization. In this case, undoubtedly dissatisfaction will increase, which will stimulate an ever-faster development outside the publicly financed part of the system. Interesting care formulas, both inside and outside the home country, will win market share and attract the most demanding customers.

Gradually, many of the employees in the public care sector will realize that there are better work conditions and more interesting customers and tasks elsewhere. An exit of customers to alternative systems will result in an exit of competent personnel. The public system will end up deeply in a vicious circle.

The *second scenario alternative* is that the publicly financed (but not necessarily publicly produced) care succeeds in recreating a strong inner dynamic that reflects the diversity of people and situations. It will profit from the opportunity revolution and increase dramatically its accessibility to citizens/customers/patients and its speed in taking care of them. This will not prevent alternative solutions from appearing, but it will clearly reduce their market. We will find less alternative and more complementary solutions.

Here is the great challenge. In a situation with so many disruptive forces that we are experiencing today, it is highly unlikely that things will remain stable. Public health systems will either plunge into a vicious circle as described above, or they will have to reconfigure themselves – and then continuous improvement along traditional lines will not be enough. Reconceptualization will be required.

This book cannot pretend to present an all-inclusive road map for the change. It strives, instead, to point at some cornerstones in such a reinterpretation, against a historical perspective and against the backdrop of how the fundamental shift to value-including welfare can be created by a system caught in the iron grip of industrial thinking.

As Lampedusa has his main character – an aristocrat facing a new era – in *Il Gattopardo* realize: 'We have to change in order to stay the same'.

2

Health care – victim of the industrial model?

Richard Normann

Environment and organization in harmony

Every organization must fit its environment. Its products and services must correspond to existing needs. Its structure and mode of functioning must correspond to the values and requirements of people, as well as to existing technology. An organization needs to change when the environment changes. Organizations strive continuously to *adapt* to new requirements of the environment.

Some organizations fail to adapt. If they operate in commercial markets they go bankrupt or they end up being acquired and reconstructed by more successful actors. If they operate

People as Care Catalysts: From being patient to becoming healthy. Edited by R. Normann and N. Arvidsson. © 2006 John Wiley & Sons, Ltd.

under conditions that depend on some other kind of support, including political, it generally takes more time before it is clear that they have failed. But sooner or later they will lose political support and support from citizens, or other participants and financiers on whom they are dependent.

In the long run, the most important process in every organization is *the ability of management to interpret the conditions and requirements of the environment, to translate them into new, sustainable values and principles of action, and then to manifest these values and principles in concrete structural manifestations* – in the organization, in management systems, new competences and new partner constellations (Figure 2.1).

Nowadays, we have learnt always to expect changes in the environment. Some changes can be regarded as *stochastic* (e.g. accidents) or *cyclical* (e.g. seasons). However, what have come to characterize the world of today, with accelerated speed since the Industrial Revolution, are the *structural* changes,

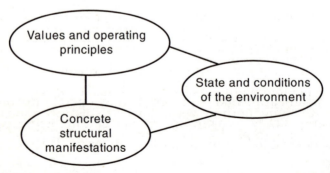

Figure 2.1 Interpretation and translation of the environmental characteristics.

i.e. changes without return to the old situation. When new structural phenomena appear in the technical area or on the demand side (e.g. drugs like Losec, gene technology breakthroughs, or HIV) there is *a need to change the very principles guiding the functioning of the system*, i.e. a restructuring.

Mankind has probably never before been faced with such strong structural changes in the environment. They are relevant everywhere and to everybody, and certainly include health care.

The industrial model: inside-out

The foundation of the industrial model is Newton's discoveries and his description of the world in a set of laws of nature, which also give the key to man not only being controlled by, but really influencing and dominating, the world. When Newton's theories eventually were translated into practical technology – e.g. James Watt's steam engine – the conditions were created for unprecedented productivity. By standardization and specialization of tasks, the assembly line came into existence. The essence of the industrial era, which succeeded the era of agriculture and craftsmanship, is summarized in the classical expression by Henry Ford: 'You can have a car in whatever color you like, as long as it is black'. Production efficiency was king; nothing was allowed to disturb standardization, resulting in productivity gains.

The European welfare states were moulded after the industrial model. There were definable and manifest needs among the people, in the form of needs for housing, remedies for widespread diseases, security in old age, etc., which could be solved by large-scale production systems and standardization. That was then.

Today's revolution: the new value creation

Information technology is without any doubt the strongest force for structural change today. In the first phase, information technology made possible a dramatic acceleration in the speed of complicated calculations and the availability of data power to everybody. It also meant that information became available to all – many information monopolies fell. In the second phase – the time of the proliferation of the Internet – completely new ways for people to communicate appeared. At the same time, complementary technologies related to search engines, database management, etc., were developed.

Thanks to the new technology, one of the old dreams of mankind has come true: the liberation of information from physical things and processes. We no longer need to 'see' things to get information about them. The information is weightlessly being transferred globally and practically at no cost. We receive information about the physical world without having to go to where the things are, and without moving the things to where we are.

The breakthrough of information technology, combined with other techniques, implies that a number of traditional restrictions to our value creation disappear. With a certain degree of simplification, it can be said that these restrictions have to do with the following:

- *Place – where we can do things.* Take the example of a home. Today it can be used not only for its traditional functions, but as a *place to work*, as a specialized *hospital* (thanks to advanced self-care systems), and even as a *prison* (using electronic foot cuffs), or as a *school* or *university*. Just to give some examples.

- *Time – when we can do things.* The fax, mobile phone and the Internet-connected portable computer make it possible for us to carry out work assignments independently of earlier existing physical time restrictions.

- *Actor – who does what?* With more information available to everyone, and with new types of appliances, we can change our roles and be released from tasks that we used to perform (e.g. going shopping – now we can order via the Internet) or make tools with the ability to help us do things we could not do earlier (e.g. performing self-diagnosis in health care). The graphics industry, for example, was somewhat shocked when Apple launched its so-called desktop publishing system, which turned all of us into graphics producers.

- *Cooperation – with whom?* New connections make competences and resources available to us globally. Today this is reflected concretely in the propagation of everything from 'chat groups' and 'Internet societies' (for example focused on a certain type of disease or state of health) to advanced systems for connecting subcontractors of, for example, a health care service.

Our first reaction is perhaps that all these trends sound nice and interesting. The deep significance of them, however, is that *they can increase, in a decisive way, the effectiveness of value creation.*[1] Thus, they make it possible, in a considerably better way than before, to use and coordinate the resources mentioned earlier, namely:

- places and infrastructures;

- time;

- competences of people;

- complementing capacities of people and other economic actors.

Let us illustrate with two examples, one that is very well known to most people, even if it is not from the health care sector, and another high technology example, which aims to change things in the health sector.

How activities that earlier were bundled together can be 'reconfigured' is illustrated by IKEA, a world leader in its industry. Figure 2.2 has been taken from their catalogue.

---

[1] By value creation we mean in the sense described by Normann (2000), i.e. value for a customer or other actor based on coproductive interaction via customer offerings. We do not refer to the commonly held notion that value creation mainly – and even only – refers to shareholder value.

This is done by IKEA:	This is done by the customer:
Design and develop the products	You check, choose and pick up the goods yourself
Wrap in flat packages	You transport the furniture to your home
Manufacture and purchase large volumes	You assemble the furniture
Check the quality and the functions	You tighten the screws
Together we save money!	

Figure 2.2 IKEA's way of organizing customers and themselves (translated from their catalogue).

What is interesting in this case is that it introduces the very idea of a company in terms of two role descriptions: the role of the company and the role of the customer. We can see that IKEA has identified and separated the different activities that are parts of the furnishing of a home, and then rearranged them along the dimensions that we have talked about:

- Regarding *place*, e.g. by moving the final assembly from a factory to the living room of the customer, for better use of the space already paid for by the customer.

- Regarding *time*, e.g. by moving the final assembly from before to after the purchase.

- Regarding *actor*, e.g. by enabling the customer to assemble the furniture, which means that a factory worker does not need to do it (and does not need to be paid by the customer for doing it).

The above-mentioned analysis only focuses on the assembly activity. However, it might also be extended to, for example, efficiency in logistics and activities that have to do with the home furnishing itself and with the selection of furniture and other utensils.

The next illustrative example is SHL Telemedicine Ltd (formerly Shahal), a company based in Israel, which also has created a unit for international expansion of its system. At the time of writing, SHL is serving over 300000 clients,[2] mainly with diagnoses like heart disease, hypertension and respiratory diseases, but also elderly people and healthy people with a high health consciousness.

The company is using online services and is based on telemedicine systems – communicating with the home of the customer (or wherever he happens to be) by mobile communication. A customer can, among other things, with the help of different sensors, measure the state of his body and send the information to monitoring centres, which are open 24 hours per day. This function is linked directly to immediate consultation and advice, based on symptoms, medical history and real-time measuring. The system is built on software developed by SHL itself, on a wide spectrum of original and advanced devices managed by the user and on systems for installation and running of telemedicine systems for home nursing.

The system creates new linkages between customers/ patients, monitoring centres, doctors, public authorities and a mobile intensive care unit. The latter consists of a fleet of intensive care equipped ambulances, each one with a doctor and paramedic plus extensive equipment for emergency care and medication.

---

[2] The firm had revenues of over 100 MUSD in 2004.

The customer offering from SHL consists of:

- an SHL monitoring centre, which communicates with the members;

- a number of disease-focused telemedicine solutions;

- online services;

- the mobile intensive care unit.

The system clearly reconfigures care. It is based on the transfer of many activities, knowledge, power and control to the customer/patient by using enabling technology, but also on better use of various other actors in and around the care system (Figure 2.3).

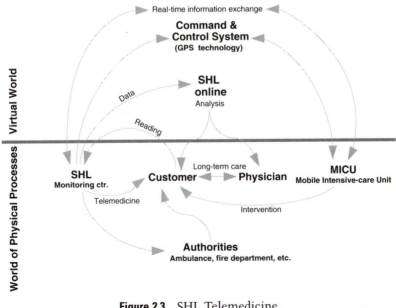

Figure 2.3   SHL Telemedicine.

The examples of IKEA and SHL are both symbols of the transfer from an industrial to a new knowledge-based and system-oriented value creation logic. Both examples imply a purely mental redefinition of a value-creating system. SHL is accomplishing this by new technology; IKEA proves that new technology is not necessary for rethinking.

Modern organizations must rethink. The industrial model must be replaced or reframed by a model where *value creation for the customers* is at the core. (For a longer discussion, see Normann, 2000.) Of course, this new model demands efficient production – as in the industrial era – and a high ability to handle relations. But the decisive competence in the new value-creating surroundings is *competence to organize value creation*. What does this mean? We can summarize in a few points (Figure 2.4):

1. Instead of being focused on a certain type of product/ service or on a certain technology, you must be focused on the customer and the customer's value creation process and on staging the value-creating meeting.

2. The competences to create *concepts* and *value-creating systems* must be developed. Competition on the markets (commercial and other) of today is not primarily about new products or services, but about the shaping of value-creating systems.

3. Instead of you yourself being the producer you have to think in terms of mobilizing those who have different types of production knowledge and products, which can be combined to form a customer offering which fits the need of the customer and his value-creating process.

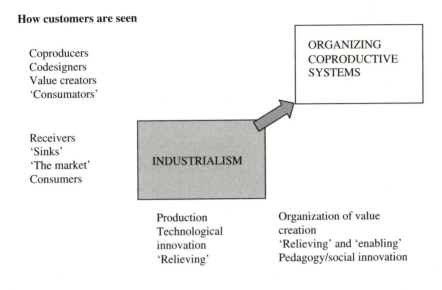

How customers are seen

Coproducers
Codesigners
Value creators
'Consumators'

ORGANIZING
COPRODUCTIVE
SYSTEMS

Receivers
'Sinks'
'The market'
Consumers

INDUSTRIALISM

Production
Technological
innovation
'Relieving'

Organization of value
creation
'Relieving' and 'enabling'
Pedagogy/social innovation

Critical competencies

Figure 2.4 View of customers and the need for critical competencies.

4. The customer must not be regarded as a 'receiver' (or a 'sink') of products you happen to have, but as a coproducer with ambitions and, not least, competence of his own and also with a dormant potential competence to participate in the value creation.

The new value creation

'Value' is not a simple or one-dimensional concept. 'Value' may refer to a physical or material standard of living, justice, aesthetics, ethics and morals, etc. 'Prosperity' and 'welfare' are notions often used to summarize several such dimensions. It is clear that value in this sense is strongly related to the economic notion of 'productivity', i.e. how efficiently resources can be mobilized and used.

Today, the most common comprehensive 'concept of value' or 'value indicator' is gross national product per capita. Even if it has its obvious shortcomings, it is still a reasonable indicator of what level of productivity has been reached and, therefore, of what the possibilities in a given society are to create value of different dimensions for its people. It is believed generally that new knowledge contributes to the creation of prosperity. Probably this is correct, but new – and potentially revolutionary – knowledge has, on many occasions, been created in Arabic countries, in China and in Europe without having deeper effects on society and the value created for people. New knowledge is a necessary, but not sufficient, prerequisite that must complement a number of other factors, such as:

- a wish and willingness to change, and openness towards new ideas in society – including political tolerance;

- a desire to invest in the future;

- acceptance of entrepreneurial values;

- institutional renewal.

These conditions have been at hand in those parts of the world that have had the best growth in value creation. For example, the Industrial Revolution was not only a technical development, but also a fundamental restructuring of the institutions of society, among companies, of political parties, of the financial sphere, of the labour market, and so on.

Technological evolution has always implied the opportunity to break out of constraints. It has become possible to produce more with fewer resources, to eliminate restrictions due to distance and time, to accumulate and preserve knowledge and build it into new systems. But technological innovation must be accompanied by social and institutional innovation if prosperity is to be realized.

Health care following business practice – but out of phase

The public service production of the European welfare model has been influenced by methods and discoveries used by industry and commerce. Against this background we will point out two important ways in which public service production, and thus health care, has tried to imitate the success formulas of business – and in both cases found out that the business community already had taken new steps. Increased awareness of these situations can help us to understand some of today's problems and how they can be eliminated in an idealized design.

Out of phase 1: an industrial model in a service era

When the big public service production systems of welfare services were built up in the European welfare model, the general opinion was that the future belonged to the industrial model. The systems were, therefore, largely built on the principles of this model: standardizing, mass production in large factories and the view of the customer as a 'receiver'. However, in business circles it has been discovered that this formula is starting to fall apart. The customer has become more powerful, and greater sensitivity, differentiated handling of differences between customers, and handling of the customer as a coproducer and not only as a receiving resource, have become imperative.

However, public service production has been left very much in the old mould. Identical treatment of everyone continues to be a word of honour, often protected by a confused reasoning about democracy. Citizens continue to be regarded, not as coproducers, but as passive receivers supposed to be satisfied with the services produced by the system.

Out of phase 2: the introduction of obsolete market mechanisms

As insight has grown into the fact that the fast speed of change of the world around us requires increased flexibility and an ability to change also from public services, including care, there have been attempts to copy another basic thought from business organizations: market mechanisms. The collapse of the state-planned economies and their inability to create value for their citizens in recent decades has, of course, strengthened this trend.

In public service production, and more particularly in care, there have been efforts to try to reflect this insight by introducing market mechanisms. We will investigate two such initiatives and show that, again, in both cases, it has been done too late.

In care, one way to reflect market mechanisms is by so-called 'privatization'. Well-defined units or parts of the care system have been detached and offered to private actors via contract-by-tender agreements. Another such mechanism is to introduce market mechanisms within the framework of the public system. This is done by the so-called 'buy–sell model'. Thus, for example, care in some Swedish regions has been reorganized into one production side and one side representing the customers. Both sides negotiate and the buying side buys services from the production side. Then these services are offered to the customers.

Today, the markets are governed by the very competence to create system solutions of known (and sometimes new) components, which are recombined. Paradoxically, one could say that the most interesting market today is about who can put the traditional market mechanisms of individual components out of play by redefining the systems. In this way, competition is between system solutions, which among themselves can be very different, and not about individual components. *Competition is about value-creating systems, not about individual products.*

Apart from this, there are of course many of the traditional markets left. When SHL built their system, they let different manufacturers of sensors, telecommunication transfer, terminals, etc., compete. But SHL competes with total system solutions in relation to the customers.

In companies it is more and more the competence to create such system solutions that is decisive. This is also reflected in their organization and mode of functioning. In a world where everything can be separated and recombined in new ways – which is typical of care – the market is about (and should be about) the ability to find effective systemic solutions, not about who creates the individual product or service at the cheapest price.

Against this background it can be established that the introduction of market mechanisms in health care is out of phase in time. It can be summarized briefly in the following way:

1. The buy–sell model tends to create a quasi-market and no real market. This is a statement that is not only a result of the reasoning above, but it is also valid in general. The customer never has a choice and no relation with any 'market'; it is only an 'internal' market between those who produce and those who buy. This looks like the Japanese keiretsu model that is disintegrating, and which is one of the reasons for the decline that the economy of Japan now is experiencing. Those who negotiate with each other have the same owner, and it is doubtful whether this is a case of a genuine market. As long as the final customer does not have any power in the marketplace, there can never be a genuine market mechanism.

2. The trend towards 'privatizing' and contract-by-tender agreements for certain units is a double-edged sword. Our experience of privatization – also from other countries and other industries – indicates that the type of contracts concerned can lead to a further staleness of the system instead

of a broader thinking about system solutions. A contract-by-tender agreement usually is about a very well-defined unit and precisely specifying what is to be produced by the unit. This preserves definitions of system borderlines and of different subsystems. It is, therefore, often counterproductive to the struggle that ought to take place in the new economy to give more room to creative redefinitions of system boundaries and configurations.

We want to stress that it is not the principle of private ownership or private operations of activities that we criticize. It is the form that generally has been taken when privatizing that we consider to be preserving the system and, therefore, blocking change.

3. The buy–sell system in reality has come to be about a market of traditional types of services and products. The system development competence has been developed but remains too low.[3]

The opportunity explosion

Health care has always evolved. It has accepted new scientific discoveries, new technologies and it has adapted to a

---

[3] A purchase of local health care, including primary, specialist and emergency care, was made in Simrishamn in Sweden in 2000. This was an original purchase because it had more of a system character than normally is the case, and since the system borderlines were defined more clearly according to the 'care logics'. Without having any detailed knowledge about the Simrishamn solution, it seems it could be a guide that indicates the direction in which future care systems could develop. We provide a detailed guide in the description of the idealized design, however.

gradually changing panorama of illnesses. However, in countries with national health care systems characterized by little
competition and few challengers to these care systems, the
underlying principles of their design have only marginally
changed in the last 50 years or so. For many reasons such
slow, marginal adaptation will not be enough. On the other
hand, in countries where market forces are playing a large role
and where the systems are fragmented – as in the US – it is
also evident that a change of principles is necessary and
possibly on its way. The points of departure are different; the
driving forces the same; the challenges for those who are to
develop new structural solutions for health care are identical.

Thus, it is not possible today – as it was at the time of the
original construction of the national care systems – to build
a once-and-for-all given model of a long-lasting stable structure. Instead, we now have to aim at constructing a health
care system with an *inherent ability for continuous self-
creation.*

The knowledge frontier is moving ahead. The revolution of
information technology is already here. Medical technology
is moving on rapidly. Pharmacology – the development of new
medicines – is progressing constantly. The revolution of
biotechnology is on its way, promoted by breakthroughs in
gene technology. Without the help of IT, it would not have
been possible to make the breakthroughs leading to an understanding of the human genetic code.

Machine technology resulted in the decrease of mankind's
earlier dependence on muscular strength. In the same way,
information technology results in the abolition of old limits

concerning time and space. Activities, which earlier could only be carried out in certain places and in a certain time sequence, can now be accomplished liberated from many of these restrictions.

We see an opportunity explosion with great consequences for the health care system – a big word, but we are convinced that it is an accurate one. New space is opening up and it is important to exploit it. It requires insight, courage and ability to change. If the public health care system does not take advantage of these possibilities, others will do it anyway and the public system will be left behind. The result will be a public system that ever increasing numbers of citizens will criticize (and for very good reasons), refuse to use and eliminate for the benefit of other solutions.

3

Who and where is the customer?

Richard Normann

From passive receiver to active coproduction

Since *the customer perspective* is particularly important in the new value creation for the new era, we feel it is important to develop this concept further. One of the characteristics of service activities – as opposed to manufacturing of goods – is that services are typically produced and used simultaneously, and the user/customer participates in the production and delivery of the service (see, for example, Normann, 2000). A consequence of this is that the quality and effectiveness of services is, to a great extent, a function of how involved and effective the customer can be made.

People as Care Catalysts: From being patient to becoming healthy. Edited by R. Normann and N. Arvidsson. © 2006 John Wiley & Sons, Ltd.

The example of IKEA, quoted earlier, is but one of many examples of how service innovation and huge leaps of effectiveness can be achieved by designing systems that call for – and enable – more active participation and coproduction by customers. This theme is further developed in Chapter 4.

Thus, there is a general trend in business to start looking at customers as *resources of value creation* and not only as passive receivers and consumers. Regarding health care, it is evident not only that this is a trend and a desire of the individuals, but also that there is an extremely big 'health-creating potential' from increased coproduction of the individual. Especially since many health problems today are related to personal lifestyles.

New technology and increased competences result in increased possibilities for coproduction. Information technology and the Internet enhance access to knowledge, create more stringent demands and lead to more educated people. Both patients and healthy people learn ever more through new technology and through (old and new) media that spread health information ever further. Thus, an increased diversity of demands on caregivers appears.

Correspondingly, higher individual coproduction leads to a need for deep knowledge of, and respect for, the individual in the system. High levels of technology and deeper personal interaction can be developed in this way, and enrich the meeting between care providers and the individual. The good motto 'hi tech–hi touch' can be realized to a large degree. This is illustrated by Figure 3.1.

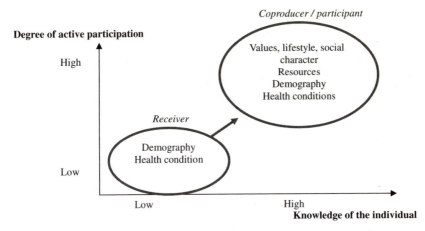

Figure 3.1 A deeper understanding of the emerging human conditions.

However, seeing the individual, both as client and more narrowly as patient, as an active *coproducer*, rather than a passive
receiver, also implies new complications. The diversity of
perspectives we have tried to demonstrate forces us to accept
that people also are different when it comes to resources of
coproduction like social networks, competences and information. Because of this, some people will ask if there is a risk of
health care becoming less equal and less democratic. The
answer is, of course, that there is such a risk, but that there still
is an inevitable and desirable trend towards the individual as a
coproducer. It would contradict all common sense to say no to
the resources that the participating individual offers. It would
also lead to a situation where the individuals most oriented
toward coproduction would look for other solutions and leave
the established system to itself.

Certain groups and individuals become pioneers and have a
diffusion effect on other groups. Apart from this, the system
is confronted with the great challenge of creating opportun-

ities for coproduction in groups that, in different aspects, are weak regarding resources. The challenges are complex and real, but many apprehensions are exaggerated and contradicted by experiences from other situations. Here are some examples of the latter:

1. Relatively small groups can often enforce large changes that are profitable to everyone within an entire system. One example of this is when regulations disappeared in the telecommunications industry. For example, when Swedish customers got the chance to choose other telephone companies than Telia (the former Swedish telecom monopoly) for less expensive international calls, only a very small proportion of all customers actually changed supplier. But these few customers, and the threat that more customers could do the same, forced Telia to lower rates drastically – which was beneficial to all customers.

2. It is sometimes maintained that, for example, very old or very sick people do not find any pleasure in Internet information. All experience implies that this is wrong. Almost everybody today has people in his or her social network – friends, children, grandchildren and others – who can access the Internet and help find information. Cases start to appear where companies or health care institutions, by connecting patients with similar symptoms and needs, become catalysts of knowledge development and activate people who otherwise would have lagged behind knowledge-wise.

To summarize, transfer of knowledge, in order to stimulate the patient/customer to learn and develop knowledge, becomes an increasing part of the relationship between the individual and the care system. With the demand for deepened relations, an increased diversification of challenges appears to caregivers.

An important digression: citizen – customer – patient; difficult but precise concepts

When we begin to discuss the relationship between the individual and the care system, linguistic difficulties soon arise. What is the role of the individual in relation to the system? Most people use, without any hesitation, the word *patients*, others use *citizens*, still others *users*, and in addition to that it is becoming more and more common to talk about *customers*. There is also a clear trend towards talking about *care consumers*.

Which word you choose to use is not only a semantic question! Hidden behind the words are different perspectives, different world views and perhaps also values. If you, as a general concept, decide on one or another, you exclude certain ways of regarding the whole care system and the relationship of the individual to this system. The three notions of *citizen*, *customer* and *patient* bring forth different aspects of the individual's relationship to care, each of them relevant, but incomplete. They supplement each other, and the exclusion of any one of them would diminish the sharpness and richness of the description of reality. Every concept brings forward a special aspect, which might be an important part of the truth – but not necessarily the whole truth.

The origin of the word 'consume' comes from Latin and originally had two different meanings. One of these roughly means 'consume', 'finish up' or 'waste'. This meaning does not seem to be an adequate concept concerning service-producing activities, where the typical situation refers to customers who not only receive, but also take part in, the production. Alvin Toffler (1980) coined the notion of *prosumer* to stress this. Intuitively, it also seems wrong to rank the individual's relationship to care in the same category as his relationship to sodas and hamburgers. The terms *users* and *receivers* can also be criticized; they imply a passive role of the person involved. The English language – as opposed to several other languages – has retained the word 'consummate' to indicate the second meaning in the Latin language. This means 'complete' or 'perfect' (as verbs) and gives a whole different connotation to the idea of what a customer does or can do.

People may be looked upon as *citizens* in two ways. As long as the care system has a strong element of political control – which is the case, even if to a varying degree, in all developed countries – we relate to care by the formal political system, for example by voting. As citizens, we also express, through the democratic process, what kind of care system and what kind of society we want, regardless of our own personal relationship to care. Secondly, as citizens, we then have the benefits and obligations of the system that has been put in place.

A completely different role of the individual in relation to the system is described by the concept of *patient* (see Figure 3.2).

The word *patient* has a multitude of meanings according to the Merriam–Webster dictionary:

1: bearing pains or trials calmly or without complaints;

2: manifesting forbearance under provocation or strain;

3: not hasty or impetuous;

4: steadfast despite opposition, difficulty or adversity;

5a: able or willing to bear (patience), used with;

5b: susceptible, admitting to (patience).

Thus, the inner meaning of the word *patient* relates to: *bearing pain without complaining or making objections.*

Figure 3.2 The meaning of *patient.*

In principle, *patient* is a term used by the care-producing professionals, who devote themselves to curing ill people. He who has an accident or becomes ill and comes into contact with the care system is the patient of the system. Nursing staff, hospitals and other care institutions work with patients on a daily basis. When, as individuals, we are ill and receive care from the system, we look upon ourselves as patients. As citizens, we have taken part in the process of influence to get a care system that can receive us as patients.

At a health care seminar in 1997, one of the authors used the notion of *customer* in a presentation. This led to an agitated letter to the editor of the Swedish *Läkartidningen*, and we were given the chance to comment on this letter. Our view of the meaning of customer is summarized in the answer, which is reproduced here:[1]

---

[1] Normann (1999). For pedagogical reasons, the word *customer* was not used in the answer. It was replaced by a meaningless word invented by a random process (*gakk*). The point was to show that a concept not covered by the

The concept of patient is not good enough. Why?

First, 'customer', as opposed to 'patient', indicates that we consider the relation to continue beyond the actual care episode.

Second, the 'patient' concept has often (not always) indicated a more narrow and diagnosis-related perspective of the individual. 'Customer' relates to a broader perspective, including a more humanistic one.

Third, the 'customer' perspective also gives an explicit focus on the health-creating – not only disease-treating – activities of the individual.

Fourth, a 'patient' as such may be quite powerless (by definition, ill). In the case of severe illness, the patient's chance of influencing the care-producing system may be non-existing. However, it is clear that nothing works like demands from users with freedom of choice in promoting innovation ability in an organization. Thus, a 'customer' is – for those who work with developing the care system – a development catalyst. Uncomfortable to those who do not like innovation – great for those who believe it is necessary.[2]

The concept of a customer to many people implies a commercial touch, which is not approved of in connection with health care. The more profound meaning of the customer concept, however, is not a commercial one, but basically signifies someone who makes demands on those who have something to offer and who has the right to do so. This aspect

---

traditional meaning of *patient* is important if we want to go ahead with the development of care. Both before and after, together with many others, we have found that there is no generally accepted word that works better than customer when it comes to the concept that needs to be illustrated. This is why we have used the word customer in the quotation here, instead of the originally used, random-process-generated word gakk.

[2] For further reading on the consumer concept see Chapter 4.

of the role of the individual in relation to the health care system must be strongly emphasized. *It is the importance of the demanding individual, his right to be demanding and the access to means to be so, that makes the customer concept, interpreted in this way, essential.* Having said this, we would love to find an alternative to the word *customer* as long as that concept continues to auto-trigger the notion of commercialism, which is not what we are trying to convey. But we have not yet succeeded.

4

The future shape of health care

Gordon Best and John Harries

Introduction and overview

This chapter uses a number of the ideas developed by Richard
Normann (2000b) to describe how health services in industrialized countries are likely to be reshaped over the coming
decade. We identify seven trends already present in the health
care 'landscape' that will be central in driving this change –
especially changes in the role users will play in 'coproducing'
many of the services they need, and in making judgements
about the acceptability and quality of these services. Three
examples are used to illustrate how these trends are already
shaping health care in ways consistent with this future.
Drawing on these examples, the chapter identifies five key
features likely to be central to a modern, enabling 21st
century health care system. Finally, this view of the future

People as Care Catalysts: From being patient to becoming healthy. Edited by
R. Normann and N. Arvidsson.   © 2006 John Wiley & Sons, Ltd.

is used to reflect and comment on some recent developments in the UK National Health Service (NHS). These developments have been characterized by the creation of a Department of Health 'Modernization Agency' (NHS Institute for Learning, Skills and Innovation) whose role is to bring about a radical reconceptualization and redesign in order to create a modernized NHS. The chapter concludes by suggesting that much of what is taking place in the UK can be described most accurately as an updating and refurbishment of the existing system, *renewing*, rather than *modernizing*, health care.

The future shape of health care

The first key idea in our discussion is the distinction Normann (2000a) makes between two types of exchange or transaction that take place between producers and consumers in all sectors of the economy:

1. Those transactions that conform to a *relieving logic*, in which the customer or user is *relieved* of the need to perform some activity for themselves by the system, which takes over this activity for them. For example, someone who is suffering from hypertension may know that they need to have their blood pressure monitored on a regular basis, but may choose to be relieved of the need to perform this activity by asking their GP to do this. In this example, an individual with a need to have his blood pressure monitored is relieved of the need to do this by his GP.

2. Those transactions that conform to an *enabling logic*, in which the customer or user is *enabled* by the transaction to create something they value. For example, someone with hypertension knowing that their blood pressure needs to be monitored might choose to purchase a home monitor in order to measure their blood pressure themselves, to understand more about their condition and, therefore, when they might need to consult their GP or other clinician. In this example, an individual with hypertension, despite having ready access to their GP, takes a decision to monitor their condition themselves so as to be in a position to decide when to involve their GP. In other words, this individual, by securing access to a home monitor, is enabled to become involved more actively in taking decisions about their condition and preferred interaction with their clinician.

Relieving means that a relatively specialized provider does things for the customer/user that the provider can do better, while *enabling* expands what a customer/user can do (as opposed to just liberating them from having to do what they did before). In this case, it is the business of the provider to deliver the *knowledge* and *tools* necessary for performing the task *per se*, which is now done by the customer (Normann, 2000a, p. 83). In general, users play a relatively passive role in transactions rooted in a relieving logic. By contrast, they play a more active, and often more creative, role when participating in transactions rooted in an enabling logic. This is the reason why Normann explicitly avoids use of the term 'consumer', since that term has the connotation of the customer as a passive receiver being relieved rather than enabled. Normann prefers to think of customers as 'value creators' rather than 'consumers'.

Normann and Ramirez (1993) use the term *coproduction* to characterize enabling transactions in which the consumer or user is engaged actively in contributing to the creation of something they value. For Normann, the notion of coproduction is not only about producers getting together to coproduce; it is about consumers or users becoming engaged in the value creation process. A classic example here is the relationship between a patient and a general practitioner (GP). Many patients visit their GP with symptoms or conditions that they do not understand fully and which are, therefore, causing them anxiety. Their GP might then examine them, carry out a few tests and then announce that they may be suffering from such and such condition but they must wait for the tests to be analysed before knowing for sure. In the interim, they may be offered a course of drugs to control or suppress the symptoms. Another GP dealing with the same patient might suggest that they visit two or three websites, where they will find information about their symptoms, the effectiveness and side effects of alternative courses of treatment and perhaps exchange views with others experiencing similar problems. The GP might then suggest that they meet again to decide together what to do next. In both cases, it is of course the intention of the GP to cure or manage the patient's distressing condition. However, in the first case, the GP acted in 'relieving' mode; in the second case, the GP acted in 'enabling' mode to equip the patient with the expertise to actively engage in the *coproduction* of the management and preferred course of treatment.

Finally, Normann, building on earlier research with Ramirez (see, for example, Normann and Ramirez, 1993), distinguishes between linear *value chains*, characteristic of the industrial economy, and *constellations of value-adding activities* that are increasingly central to the post-industrial economy (Normann and Ramirez, 1993, pp. 49–59). Implicit in the idea of a value chain is the assumption that producers produce (goods or services), and customers consume. By contrast, the notion of value-adding constellations draws attention to the fact that in a post-industrial economy, the critical competence is already, and will increasingly be, the organization of value creation – often involving the customer (who is increasingly no longer simply a consumer) as coproducer.

Figure 4.1 illustrates how these ideas might be used to begin thinking about the future shape of health care. The horizontal axis of Figure 4.1 denotes the role of the health care system (i.e. hospitals, clinics, clinicians, pharmacies, etc.) as a

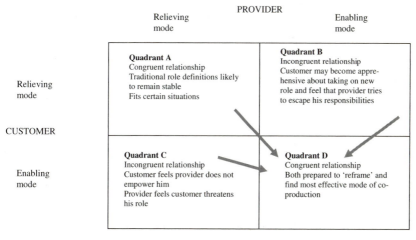

Figure 4.1 Customers and providers.

'producer' of services or activities that impact on health and wellbeing. These range from a series of essentially relieving transactions (R) on the left of the axis, across to more enabling transactions (E) on the right of the axis. The vertical axis denotes the same principle but for the users (or clients or patients) of the system, ranging from those who might be in 'relieving' mode or who are simply unable to perform the necessary activities for themselves (top of the axis), to those who might need or want to be 'enabled'.

More specifically:

- *Quadrant A* (i.e. relieving–relieving) might include someone who has been in a car accident, has a badly fractured skull and needs treatment (i.e. the condition forces them into a relieving mode because they are simply unable physically to contribute in any way to their treatment). If the health care system is working well, the hospital neurosurgeon and other staff will engage in activities that address the person's condition and relieve them of any immediate role in their own treatment. So the patient needs to be relieved and the neurosurgeon obliges. This is that part of the health care system often referred to as the *illness service*; in general, it conforms to what Normann would call a relieving logic.

- *Quadrant B* (i.e., relieving–enabling) might include a client who wants, or believes they need, to be relieved of the need to manage their own condition, but where they probably can be helped best through enabling. Many psychiatric clients and many individuals suffering from substance or other forms of abuse are often located in this quadrant. For example, an individual suffering from disabling anxiety may seek to be relieved of the need to cope with their condition by the prescription of drugs. However, good clinical practice may indicate that they can be helped best if they are enabled by, for example, learning techniques for managing panic attacks. There may, thus, be a lack of congruence between the relieving mode of the patient and the enabling mode of the practitioner. As a result there may be a tendency to end up in Quadrant A, whereas they need to be helped to move to Quadrant D.

- *Quadrant C* (i.e. enabling–relieving) includes those clients who want to be enabled to participate more actively in maintaining and/or restoring their health and wellbeing, but where the services offered by the health care system are rooted in a relieving logic. The classic example here is the expectant mother who wishes to participate actively in the birth of her child by, for example, giving birth at home so that she has greater control over the environment within which delivery takes place, but where the system offers only hospital deliveries. Unlike Quadrant B, where the client desires relief but can probably only benefit from enabling, clients in Quadrant C want to be enabled but, often, are only relieved of the contribution they wish to make (i.e., they are dealt with in Quadrant A, whereas ideally they should be empowered to move into Quadrant D).

- *Quadrant D* (i.e. enabling–enabling) includes those clients who wish, or need, to be enabled to participate more actively in maintaining and/or restoring their health and wellbeing, and who are empowered to do so. Examples here would include elderly people who work with domiciliary and district nursing staff to 'coproduce' living at home; parents who work with nursing and other staff to 'coproduce' hospital care for their children; and an individual working through the Internet and with their primary care clinician to 'coproduce' a diagnosis and management of their condition. The best health promotion programmes are also located in this quadrant.

The grey arrows in Figure 4.1 denote the broad direction health care reform will need to take if it is to lead to a truly modernized, enabling health care system. Thus, the arrow pointing from Quadrant A to D is meant to suggest that those activities rooted in a relieving logic (i.e. in Quadrant A), while important, should only attract investment if they are both appropriate and effective; where they are not, they should be supplemented or replaced by enabling activities located in Quadrant D. The arrows pointing from Quadrants B and C to Quadrant D are meant to suggest that many transactions presently (and often inappropriately) rooted in a relieving logic (either because that is what the user seeks and/or that is what the system is prepared to offer) should be minimized and, where practical, replaced by transactions rooted in an enabling logic within Quadrant D. The examples given below illustrate how these shifts are already taking place in health care systems throughout the Western world.

If Figure 4.1 describes the broad direction reform is likely to take, the seven trends shown in Figure 4.2 describe some of the key features of the health care 'landscape' that will determine just how this direction is likely to be realized in practice.

1. **The acute 'episode' will become increasingly targeted**: i.e., more things are happening to patients before they enter an acute episode (e.g. preventative drug regimes) and more things happen to them afterwards (e.g., 'step down' care). These activities sometimes make the inpatient episode unnecessary; in many cases they make the episode shorter; in come cases they make 'self care' practical.

2. **There will be increasing investment in, and much more varied forms of, 'gate keeping'**: i.e., an increasingly wide range of clinical practitioners are playing gate keeping roles. This often means that if and when patients receive care, it is more closely tailored to their needs; it sometimes means that the 'diagnosis' is brought to the patient (rather than the other way around); and it increasingly means that patients are actively involved in coproducing their own diagnosis and treatment protocols.

3. **There will be a simultaneous growth in both generalization and specialization**: i.e., the roles and responsibilities of clinical generalists are expanding to encompass more and more aspects of patient liaison and management. Simultaneously, clinical specialists are becoming more and more specialized and increasingly operate only in acute high-tech settings. The former trend offers greater scope for patients/users to coproduce their care, while the latter trend means that the illness service is increasingly focused on those who need it.

4. **More doctors and other clinical specialists will work outside institutions**: i.e., as advances in information, medical and telemedicine technology free the practice of medicine from the constraints of time and location, more and more high-tech medicine is taking place outside hospitals. This again offers greater scope for patients/users to participate more actively in their own care – often in home settings.

5. **There will be an increase in 'capitated' forms of funding**: i.e., as the pressures to contain escalating costs grow, more and more health care is being funded on a cash-limited, capitated basis. This introduces incentives that motivate clinicians (and others) to target more carefully the care they offer.

6. **Consumers and users will play a much more active role in 'clinical' decision making**: i.e., higher consumer expectations, combined with the ready availability of medical information and knowledge via the Internet, mean that users of the health care system want (and are increasingly qualified) to play a more central role in determining when, where and how they receive care and who their partners are in providing it.

7. **Developments in genomics, nanotechnology, pharmacology and information technology will make the future more 'fluid' and increasingly impossible to predict**: i.e., these developments mean that the world of health care is becoming increasingly 'dematerialized'. Freed from the constraints of time and place, this means that an increasing number of health care activities can be 'unbundled' and 'rebundled' in ways that achieve greater cost effectiveness, are more convenient and/or are more closely tailored to the needs of the patient/user as an individual.

Figure 4.2 Seven trends that will determine the future shape of health and social care.

The implications from the seven trends suggest:

- The growth in capitated funding and the search for greater cost-effectiveness will mean that *there will be increasing pressure to limit access to the institutionalized acute sector to those patients that clearly need, and can clearly benefit from, this form of care* (the small arrows in

Quadrant A of Figure 4.1 denote these pressures). These pressures have their origins in trends 1, 2, 4 and 5 of Figure 4.2).

- The expanding role of the generalist clinician and the rapid growth in 'enabling' technology will mean that there will be more and more opportunities for *patients/users to be active partners in their own care and to have greater influence over where, when and how they receive and/or coproduce the care they need* (trends 3, 6 and 7).

- The rapid growth in information, telemedical and medico-pharmacological technology will mean increasingly that *many health care activities will no longer be tied to a specific time, place or practitioner. In addition, many activities will become 'dematerialized' (Normann, 2000b, p. 30) and therefore able to be 'rebundled' in different forms; as a result, they will become much more susceptible to the preferences and control of the patient/user* (trends 3, 6 and 7).

Indeed, as the illustrations above suggest, there are numerous examples of existing and emerging forms of health care delivery that are consistent with the direction implied by the grey arrows in Figure 4.1 and the trends summarized in Figure 4.2. While little of the foregoing may be novel, the explosive increase in scientific innovation and new technology means that the opportunities to move in these directions are likely to proliferate dramatically over the next decade. Moreover, as these opportunities present themselves, so too will opportunities to reconfigure the health care system in ways that place the user at the centre of 'constellations of value-creating activities' (Normann, 2000b, pp. 24–25), where they will be enabled to play a more active role in determining how services are accessed, in the coproduction of many services and activities and in making judgements about the acceptability and quality of services. The next section takes a closer look at what this is likely to mean in practice.

The emerging health care landscape: some examples

Reconfiguration does not just happen. As new (technological and other) opportunities arise to reshape the business landscape, new (value creation) *rules* often come into play and new (redesigned) *competencies* must be developed in order to play successfully by these new rules. Individuals and organizations that learn quickly how to play by these rules and therefore, like IKEA, reconfigure the business landscape successfully, have been described as *prime movers* (Normann, 2000b, pp. 61–88). Although there is much more to be said on the subject of reconfiguring value-creating activities, it may, nevertheless, be useful to use this simple framework to examine three examples of the reconfiguration of health care delivery.

Example 1 – Reconfiguring support for the elderly

Kaiser Permanente is one of the oldest prepaid managed care plans in the United States. As a consequence, they cater for a population that, on average, is probably somewhat older than that enrolled in most such plans. Not surprisingly, this means that they are experiencing some of the sociomedical problems often associated with elderly populations. For example, about two years ago they became preoccupied with the increasing number of elderly people arriving in their primary care and outpatient clinics as well as in the casualty departments of their hospitals. Many of these people required little, if any, medical care, but instead required various forms of reassurance, 'social' support and information. Kaiser Permanente's facilities, however, were geared up to provide services that were suited to transactions rooted in a relieving logic (i.e., various forms of medical diagnosis and treatment). They were, therefore, very poorly placed to offer the support most of these people needed.

A group of Kaiser Permanente's geriatricians who were aware of this problem decided to tackle it in a very different way. They decided to hold a monthly 'group clinic' for all of Kaiser Permanente's members who were over the age of 70, had attended one or more of their outpatient clinics or casualty departments in the past 12 months and had, at the time of their attendance, been judged to require little or no medical care. All of KP's members falling into this category were duly contacted and asked to attend a monthly 'clinic' where they could take coffee and refreshments, play cards and other games, make use of a community library, watch a video, talk, if they so wished to a doctor, nurse or other clinician, and so on. While this was going on, the small number of clinicians present maintained a low profile, observing carefully and, where judged appropriate, perhaps suggesting a minor medical 'intervention,' such as a dosage adjustment for an existing prescription or attendance at an outpatient clinic at a future date.

Within a short time, most of those attending the monthly group clinic began to strike up friendships that resulted in the formation of social networks, enabling members to offer one another various types of support between clinics. This ranged from simple telephone contact to social engagements involving groups of members taking part in similar activities to those offered at the group clinic. Not surprisingly, the attendance of those aged over 70 at Kaiser Permanente's outpatient and other clinics showed a steady and significant decline. These elderly people had been *enabled* to participate actively in maintaining their health and wellbeing; they no longer felt the 'need' for relief. In addition, this new arrangement allowed clinicians to make more effective use of their time. Rather than dealing with these individuals as 'patients' in a setting designed to offer treatment, the group clinics provided an environment in which clinicians were able to make more 'rounded' judgements reflecting both the clinical and social needs of these individuals.

In Normann's terms this constitutes an example of 'reconfiguring value-creating systems', in that the enabling mode adopted by Kaiser Permanente resulted in these elderly people creating a network of individuals who, in various ways, could provide mutual support. This network enhanced their sense of wellbeing and security in ways that could not have been achieved by Kaiser Permanente's traditional systems of care. Kaiser Permanente's geriatricians had reconfigured the 'health and social care landscape' so as to offer something that responded to the 'unexpressed need' of the elderly people. In terms of Figure 4.1, this is an example of making more effective use of the resources located in Quadrant A, while moving some activities from Quadrants A and C to Quadrant D. Table 4.1 illustrates how the Normann framework sketched out above can be used to understand this example in further depth.

Example 2 – Reconfiguring orthopaedic rehabilitation

One of the chronic problems contributing to the mis-utilization of acute beds in NHS hospitals (and probably acute hospitals in many other countries) is the need to help many patients following major surgery (e.g. hip, knee replacement) to become mobile before they can be discharged safely, and the relatively high readmission rates of such patients following accidents or other mishaps during the home-based rehabilitation period. The first part of the problem arises because these patients often need to develop the competencies and confidence to use unfamiliar aids, such as crutches or walking frames, safely. The latter part of the problem often arises either because the pressure on acute beds is such that patients are discharged before they are fully competent to use their new aids, and/or because conditions at home are such that what they have learned in the hospital is inadequate to cope with their new surroundings.

In a number of NHS hospitals, multidisciplinary teams of orthopaedic surgeons and nurses, hospital-based rehabilitation therapists, community nurses and therapists, as well as local authority housing staff, have instituted a new regime in

Table 4.1 Reconfiguring support for the elderly

Group clinic for the elderly	Old	New
Where things can happen	Outpatients Dept (OPD); Accident & Emergency (A&E) Dept.	Group clinic; individuals' homes.
When they can happen	Upon arrival at OPD or A&E.	Monthly and/or as invited by peers.
Who can do what?	Professional specialist(s).	Professional generalist(s) and/or peers.
With whom it can be done	Professionals available in hospital setting.	Generalists in group clinic; peers in group clinic and/or in individuals' homes.
New rules	(i) Client's peers can provide care. (ii) Clients often need support not 'cure'. (iii) Support can reduce the demand for care. (iv) The 'gate keeping' function can be carried out by different individuals in different locations. (v) Whole-person observation can influence diagnosis.	
New competencies and emphasis	(i) Creating congenial, multifunctional environments – i.e. 'empathic' design skills. (ii) Facilitating the creation of 'patient' networks and communities. (iii) Developing informal modes of 'diagnosis'. (iv) Managing demand through dealing with the 'patient' as a whole person/individual. (v) Orchestrating new constellations (i.e. combinations of people, organizations and technology) of value.	

which much rehabilitative training and care for these patients takes place *before* admission to hospital. The patients' homes are inspected prior to admission to identify and deal with potential hazards that might serve to interfere with the successful use of new mobility aids. Under these schemes, virtually all of the training in the use of crutches or other aids takes place in the patient's home (which, after all, is where they will have to use them) before admission to hospital. In addition, rehabilitative therapists inspect these patients' homes to check on hazards (e.g. loose carpets) known to have caused accidents (and therefore readmissions to hospital) in the past. In this way, patients are enabled to return home sooner and, as a result, to regain their mobility and independence more rapidly than would otherwise be the case.

Schemes such as these have served to reduce the length of hospital stay for many patients with these conditions, as well as cutting down on the readmission rates associated with post-operative accidents and mishaps. In terms of Figure 4.1, this example again represents the more efficient and effective use of those resources within Quadrant A, as well as moving some activities from both Quadrants A and B to Quadrant D. Table 4.2 provides a summary of how this example can be analysed using the framework introduced earlier.

Example 3 – Reconfiguring the acute ambulatory care interface

This example is drawn from Normann (2000b, p. 63) and is based on SHL Ltd, an Israeli organization specializing in 'online' diagnosis and ambulatory and home care services. In

Table 4.2 Reconfiguring orthopaedic rehabilitation

Orthopaedic rehabilitative care	Old	New
Where things can happen	In the hospital.	At home.
When they can happen	Following the acute episode.	Prior to the acute episode.
Who can do what?	Hospital staff.	Community nurse, occupational therapists.
With whom it can be done	Ward nurses; ambulance staff; rehabilitation therapists.	Community-based nurses and therapists; family members; friends.
New rules		(i) Rehabilitation can precede the acute episode, i.e., can be proactive rather than reactive. (ii) The demand for care can sometimes be managed through the management of the domestic environment. (iii) Family members (and friends) can be important providers of rehabilitative care. (iv) Effecting a sustained improvement in the quality of a client's life almost always requires team work, both within and outside the 'clinical community'.
New competencies and emphasis		(i) Redesigning learning processes. (ii) Domestic risk assessment. (iii) 'Empathic' planning and design skills. (iv) Orchestrating new constellations (i.e., combinations of people, organizations and technology) of value.

early 2000, SHL had approximately 55000 members, representing primarily cardiac, hypertensive and respiratory illnesses, but also elderly people and healthy people with a high level of health awareness. The services SHL offers to its members include:

- A monitoring service which can be 'online' 24 hours a day, linked to immediate consultation and advice.

- A number of disease-focused telemedicine solutions.

- A mobile intensive care unit equipped for emergency treatment and staffed by a physician, paramedic and driver-medic.

- Long-term home care arrangements.

- 24-hour links to public services such as the ambulance service, the fire department, etc.

The company uses online services and is based on telemedicine brought to the customer's home (or wherever the customer is) via mobile communications. Customers make measurements of body signals, which are then sent to the monitoring centres. These are linked to immediate consultation and advice, based on symptoms, medical history and real-time measurements. The system as a whole creates new linkages between patients/users, the monitoring centre, physicians, public authorities and a mobile intensive care unit. As Normann (2000b) puts it 'The system . . . clearly reconfigures health care. For one thing, it is explicitly based on shifting more activities, knowledge, control and power to the end-customer/patient through the use of enabling technology.'

Whereas the earlier examples illustrated how reconfiguration can take the form of relocating and rebundling existing and new activities in both time and place, exploiting existing technologies, the SHL example above illustrates clearly how the availability of new technology can open up the reconfiguration 'opportunity space' by dismantling the boundaries of the physical world and reassigning responsibilities across professional and functional boundaries. In terms of Figure 4.1, the SHL experience illustrates the reconfiguration of resources and activities in Quadrant A, as well as a shift in activity from Quadrants A, B and C to Quadrant D. Table 4.3 analyses the acute ambulatory care example using the framework introduced in this chapter.

Modernizing health care

These three examples – support for the elderly, orthopaedic rehabilitation and acute ambulatory care – provide clear illustrations of some of the different ways in which the seven trends summarized earlier present opportunities and imperatives that can often be exploited and/or harnessed by prime movers to reconfigure the health care landscape and to move closer to a genuinely modern, enabling health care system. A number of themes emerge from these examples, including:

- Peer support and self-care is often more appropriate and can replace many of the 'relieving' activities that take place typically in the acute sector.

Table 4.3 Reconfiguring the acute ambulatory care interface

SHL ambulatory care	Old	New
Where things can happen	Hospital Outpatients Dept (OPD); Accident & Emergency (A&E) Dept.	At home; monitoring centre; in mobile intensive care (IC) unit.
When they can happen	Upon arrival at OPD or A&E.	On demand; in response to monitoring signals.
Who can do what?	Professional specialist(s).	Professional generalist(s).
With whom it can be done	Specialists available in hospital setting.	Generalists and specialists in homes, monitoring centres, mobile IC units.
New rules	(i) Patients can 'orchestrate' care from a variety of locations. (ii) High technology care can be available 24 hrs a day outside hospitals. (iii) The appropriate use of new high technology may help to contain costs. (iv) Technology-dependent diagnosis, rehabilitation and long-term care can co-exist to the mutual benefit of each.	
New competencies and emphasis	(i) Systems design integrating information, telemedicine and medical technologies. (ii) Development of patient/user enabling technology. (iii) Working through and across traditional physical, functional and professional boundaries. (iv) Orchestrating new constellations (i.e. combinations of people, organizations and technology) of value.	

- New technology is making it increasingly feasible to dismantle physical, functional and professional boundaries.

- The expressed demand for health care can sometimes be managed, and the unexpressed demand and opportunities for reconfiguration can sometimes be identified and addressed, by seeing and dealing with patients/users as complete individuals.

- There is considerable scope to substitute the skills and knowledge of professional generalists for those of professional specialists if the latter are able to adopt an enabling mode and to develop the pedagogy and other enabling tools and competences.

- These developments and others mean that it is increasingly possible to make more efficient and effective use of those expensive resources that reside largely in the acute sector, while simultaneously placing the users at the centre of a constellation of activities within which they are offered greater choice and enabled to have greater control over outcomes.

What then do these arguments and examples tell us about the future shape of health care? More specifically, what do they suggest will be the key features of a truly modern, enabling health care system? Some of these are likely to be:

- *One in which every significant stakeholder institution is encouraged to adopt a prime mover mind set.* This entails understanding the larger context of service delivery and customer values and trying to envision a future for the larger system by creating, or contributing to, a design 'vision', which addresses dissatisfactions with the current system and exploits the opportunity space created by emerging technologies and competencies. 'If one's current *operational* position can be clearly defined, one's *intellectual* position must be much wider' (Normann, 2000b, p. 80).

In the commercial environment, effective prime movership is a powerful competitive advantage that can lead to the reconfiguration of systems, to the benefit of the prime mover, and the relegation of other providers within the system to the status of subcontractors or commodities (Normann, 2000b, p. 68). Cultivation of a prime movership mind set thus becomes a core competitive competency. In the public sector, by contrast, the objective in developing the prime mover state of mind is not to initiate a competitive battle in which everyone tries to raise his or her status and reconfigure everyone else. Rather, the objective is to engage the *system* in the creation of a design vision, which recognizes the interrelationships within the system and avoids the optimization of some components at the expense of others to the overall detriment of the user. To achieve such a mind set, a variety of interventions have been deployed in the British system, including Soft Systems Analysis, Systems Dynamics, Whole Systems Approaches and Scenario-based and Computerized Systems Simulations. As illustrated earlier and discussed below, the unifying design principle around which the system needs to configure is the user's experience as they navigate through it.

- *One in which service delivery organizations develop the skills of 'empathic design'.* This entails a continuous process of service innovation, driven by a systematic exploration of the values and objectives of service users in 'real' social contexts. To exploit the prime mover mind set, delivery organizations need to see themselves, not just as providers of service outputs, but as providers of input to the value creation processes of their customers. For instance, had the orthopaedic rehabilitation team in Example 2 above been unable to imagine, and then understand, what the process of home-based, post-operative recovery meant for 'real' individuals living in different 'real' home circumstances, it is unlikely that they would have ever moved beyond the idea of a 'one size fits all', hospital-based approach to rehabilitative care. The importance of user-focused empathic design increases as new opportunities arise for the empowerment of the user through the deployment of new technologies and processes. Only by adopting such an approach can genuinely innovative offerings be designed that create real value for the user.

- *One in which the boundaries of organizations and service delivery are more malleable and less worthy of respect.* This may involve the subjugation of the current mission of the organizational entity to the future vision of the system. Moreover, as long as status, salary and power is resident in organizationally bound roles, the organization is likely to remain a deeply conservative influence on systems reconfiguration. As long as finite resources are distributed to organizations according to their outputs and within a closed, zero sum game, then organizations will defend themselves at the expense of the system. Think back to the SHL example: had those responsible for developing the SHL approach to ambulatory care not had the mind sets of prime movers, it is very unlikely that an online monitoring centre, a mobile intensive care unit, telemedicine facilities and a variety of community services, all provided by separate organizations and/or delivered by staff working to autonomous budgets and financial targets, would ever have been conceived as a part of the same 'seamless', enabling service.

- *One in which the service user is stimulated and 'taught' by the offering to enable their own health-creating contribution and that of their social network.* Without this pedagogical component to the offering, users will define their service expectations in terms of traditional outputs. They may, thus, be suspicious of, and fail to exploit, the enabling characteristics of the offering. Imagine, for example, an elderly person attending a Kaiser Permanente outpatient clinic being told by the attending physician that what they needed was a 'good game of cards with some friends'! No doubt, and with good reason, they would be suspicious of this unfamiliar 'output' of the health care system. Until such time as their attendance at the group clinic had 'taught' them that a game of cards with peers might be one contribution (i.e. input) to their wellbeing, such an offering would understandably be seen as irrelevant to their perceived needs. Good offerings 'link in with the current natural processes of the user, stimulating him to do things which he was not able to do previously, but still within the natural operational and evolutionary "flow" of the user' (Normann, 2000b, p. 119).

- *One in which the key performance metrics, on which managerial and political performance are judged, reflect the extent to which the service has contributed to more subtle and user-centred value creation* as described above. In practice this implies:

  —Extending the boundaries of the measured system to include the value-creating activities of its users. In effect, taking the same perspective on the wider system as that of its prime movers.

  —Viewing the effectiveness of professional and organizational activity in terms of its input to the wider system, rather than as isolated outputs.

  —Ascribing value to, and defining metrics around, the users' experience of the system and its effectiveness in promoting their value-creating agenda.

In the SHL example discussed earlier, traditional operational metrics such as the responsiveness and utilization of the mobile intensive care unit and the reliability and uptime of remote monitoring services would be measured. However, in addition, the users' experience of the service would be assessed in terms of their sense of wellbeing, security and ability to work and engage socially. As the system shifts more activities, knowledge, control and power to the end customer/patient, its success in achieving these objectives would also need to be evaluated by identifying directly relevant metrics or proxies for these behavioural changes.

It is impossible to predict the future shape of health care in any detail. What seems clear is that the opportunities to reshape and reconfigure the health care system have never been greater and are likely to increase dramatically over the next decade. In so far as this is so, the five developments just described – i.e. the development of a prime mover mind set, empathic design skills, the capacity and imagination to dismantle boundaries, the design of 'pedagogic' offerings and the development of systemic and behavioural metrics to gauge performance – are likely to be central to our ability to exploit these opportunities and, therefore, our capacity to create a truly modern and enabling health care system.

Conclusion: a view from the UK

Like health services in most other industrialized countries, those in the United Kingdom are under a variety of pressures. These include increasing citizen dissatisfaction with the National Health Service (NHS), increasing evidence of unacceptable variations in the quality of care available to patients in different parts of the country, a crumbling and inadequate physical infrastructure and the need to improve effectiveness while controlling costs. These and other pressures have prompted a wide range of Government initiatives, including a greater emphasis on performance targets designed to improve access, enhance and standardize service quality and improve 'customer friendliness'; a major building and infrastructure upgrading programme; a series of structural changes designed to enhance the role of primary care clinicians in service commissioning, improve communications and facilitate performance monitoring; a beefed up regulatory structure to monitor cost-effectiveness and to identify and disseminate best practice; and a major staff recruitment and training programme to address service 'bottle necks' and other problems arising from staff shortages. The UK Government has described these initiatives as its plan to 'modernize' the NHS.

Looked at in the light of Figure 4.1, this is a very special, and indeed somewhat limited, use of the word 'modernization'. More specifically:

- The great majority of the above changes are focused on upgrading and improving services located in Quadrant A of Figure 4.1.

- Although there are a limited number of initiatives located in Quadrants B, C and D (e.g. the introduction of patient advocates, the introduction of 24-hour telephone access to specially trained nurse practitioners), most of these initiatives are designed to address dissatisfaction with the services in Quadrant A.

- The overriding emphasis is on improving the efficiency, effectiveness and customer friendliness of existing models of service delivery with little evidence that the UK Government (or, for that matter, most of its critics) wishes to exploit the opportunities offered by the trends in Figure 4.2 to reconfigure health care for the 21st century.

One development that could prove an exception to this is the UK Government's decision to make public the performance of surgical institutions. This has raised a number of questions about how these numbers could be interpreted meaningfully and acted upon by service users given the complexity of the issues in relation to case mix, differing characteristics of local catchment populations and the limitations imposed by the UK gate keeper/referral model. However, if the publication of such measures is intended to allow users to exercise influence and choice in relation to service delivery organizations, this could presage a new spirit of openness and engagement with the public. This in turn, could lead to the next and more fundamental level of coproduction, in which users are engaged, not just in influencing where, when and with whom they receive services, but also in the design and the delivery of the services that address their needs. To enable such a codesign process to be initiated, however, metrics would need to be created which gave meaningful information on the performance of the relevant health care systems (not just institutions, procedures and clinicians) and which allowed users, as well as professionals, to infer new and more effective delivery configurations. This is the future. To date, the UK Government – like governments in most other industrialized countries – has shown little inclination to move beyond the publication of comparative measures of performance, which may or may not enable the public to make better use of the services already on offer.

This is not to belittle nor dismiss the efforts by the UK Government to improve the National Health Service. This is what most citizens in the UK want the Government to do. At the same time, this voter attachment to the familiar is a powerful electoral constraint: i.e., while all national governments are, by definition, potential prime movers in the public service 'marketplace', it is very risky for them to exploit this role to 'reconfigure' services and thereby to introduce new and unfamiliar offerings. It is, rather, much safer to upgrade and improve the familiar, rather than run the risks of offering people something of which they have little or no experience. *In other words, it is politically safer to 'renew' rather than modernize health care.* This may be less true in countries where the government does not play such a prominent role in the funding and provision of health care, although here too, there are risks in offering existing or potential customers unfamiliar experiences – especially where these are to do with their health or the health of their loved ones.

Although the forces to renew, rather than modernize, health care are powerful in all industrialized countries, the trends summarized in Figure 4.2 will mean that the opportunities to reconfigure and create 21st century health care will go on increasing. As a consequence, and as the examples above make clear, prime movers will emerge to reshape the prevailing health care landscape. Moreover, successful prime movers will carry users and patients (and therefore voters and customers) with them. As a consequence, two key questions emerge as central to the modernization debate. First, are the risks associated with the prime movership role such that governments and other key players in health care have little choice but to pursue relatively safe options for reform, while reacting as best they can to the sovereign initiatives of those prime movers that will invariably emerge in the marketplace? Or, can governments and other key players devise more proactive strategies for encouraging and harnessing the efforts of prime movers in reconfiguring health care for the 21st century?

5

A French exception or a demonstration of a European trend?

Michel Crozier

THE FRENCH HEALTH SYSTEM IS A VERY SPECIAL CASE, IN as much as it maintains and seeks to conciliate opposing principles and yet seems to work well enough that the World Health Organization described it, in 2000, as the most efficient in the world. It is, therefore, an interesting case reflecting some vital issues – especially how industrial business logic influences health care systems – discussed in this book. It is a very fragile system, since it has been continuously in financial crisis during the last 20 years. Its basic compromise, the 'tiers payant' (third party payer), has become more and more inflationary in a period of rapid growth. As a result, acceptable regulations can neither be found nor imposed.

People as Care Catalysts: From being patient to becoming healthy. Edited by
R. Normann and N. Arvidsson. © 2006 John Wiley & Sons, Ltd.

A special case

To understand the French health system, one must return to its beginnings and the principles on which it was founded. Social security was developed in the thirties, in a period of economic disaster, over a compromise between trade unions and employers' associations, sponsored by the French State. It was completely reorganized and restructured into a comprehensive national system in 1945. Every worker was to be affiliated and sums were to be deducted from the workers' salaries. Employers would have to match these deductions as well. The huge sums generated were managed by 'Caisses régionales' (regional agencies), whose boards were elected by representatives of the employers and of the employees. These boards were generally taken over by a coalition of moderate trade unions and the employers' associations. They became a very important stronghold for the Force Ouvrière (FO) first, and then for the Confederation Democratique du Travail (CFDT). Elections to these boards, however, generated less and less attention. Abstentions gradually became more numerous. And, although the jobs they provided were crucial for the moderate labour movements, they did not carry a democratic stature. The caisses did not have much leeway. They were in charge of a huge bureaucratic establishment of white-collar workers, whose responsibility was to process the reimbursement of the printed forms emanating from the entire population. This could only have a small impact on health policy, such as by directing some social and medical actions.

For doctors and patients, the system was very simple. Patients had complete freedom in choosing whichever medical practitioners they wished to consult; they would pay them directly and be reimbursed by sending the formulas signed by the doctors to the caisse. This meant the preservation of the tradition of complete freedom of the medical profession and of the patients that was the first principle of the 'colloque singulier' (private doctor/patient relationship) on which the system was built. Such a system gave satisfaction to the main stakeholders. It offered patients (the customers of the health system) free access, without any restrictions. It gave physicians an unlimited market to which to offer their services. Trade unions were secure as indispensable go-betweens. Employers were critical of the growing costs, but could prevent too much waste while at the same time making important deals with moderate union leaders. The State guaranteed the system and controlled it. It was performing its role of peacemaker and could remain politically neutral.

This very complex system was well balanced for twenty-five years, more or less. Its complexity gave it great strength and now gives it an extraordinary resistance to change. Its values are those of the majority of French people: equality of access of all citizens to health as a major good; privacy of care relationships with the practitioners; freedom of action of the citizens, as well as the freedom of the major players, everything under State protection.

This equilibrium and the consensus that goes with it have been gradually shaken by long-term trends that have accelerated. First of all, the pressure of the financial burden originally was alleviated by the relative reluctance of the people of the less affluent classes to utilize the benefits of the system. But gradually this difference has disappeared, which has greatly increased the costs. The success of the system has increased the concern of citizens on issues pertaining to health, and this has put a growing burden on the system.

Second, the ageing of the population has changed its balance. The number of paying members – the salaried workers – has remained stable, while the number of non-payers, who at the same time are also the main source of spending, has increased the overall burden on the system.

Third, the increasing use of high technology in medicine and surgery has also increased the costs, especially in the best teaching hospitals. Accelerated progress may have helped diminish the costs of some aspects of care, but the enormous costs of the major new technologies and of medical research have made it impossible to stop the inflationary spending.

Major problems

Problems occur as a direct consequence of the principles and major compromises of the system, when the pressures of a fast-changing society make these more and more inadequate. Three main domains are presently at stake: they concern liberal practitioners, hospitals and health care policy.

For liberal practitioners, the problem shifted from entry into the profession, to the decline of the general practitioner, to the tariff of the acts and the management of the reimbursements.

In the beginning there was an informal numerus clauce to enter the profession. The 1968 student revolt suppressed it, bringing a great influx into the profession. This was followed by restrictions and disaffection for the profession, which brings France to the same level as other Western democracies, with a growth of practitioners, especially in the hospitals, coming from the third world to take over these jobs.

The basic demographic problem, however, has now become the distribution of the practitioners across the territory, between urban and rural areas, and between generalists and specialists.

The last emergence of discontent concerns the payment of the fees. It is the result of statewide negotiation between the unions of practitioners and the social security system under the supervision of the State. Strikes and demonstrations, for the first time, have taken place on a large scale. Practitioners complain about the stress of overwork and the lack of time to do fruitful work.

The management of the social security system, finally, is under attack because of the cost and burden of its paperwork. A new system involving a social security card should have replaced much of the paperwork, but because of the resistance of the employees and their unions and the practitioners' lack of interest, it is still not yet fully operational.

The problem is much more acute for the hospitals. It is in the hospitals, of course, that the cost of technical progress has been more severe. It has been compounded by the extraordinary difficulty of modernizing hospital management. There is an important group of private hospitals, but the great majority of hospitals are public. They are important employers locally, and the pressures on politicians to maintain their presence is strong. But the main difficulties come from the dual nature of management. Directors are State administrators who are recruited by competitive exams and who depend on the State to appoint and promote them. Heads of the medical teams are prestigious specialists who have easy access to the State and to the media. The war between the two potential leaders is permanent and weakens leadership.

This is compounded by the hierarchical nature of the hospital system. At the apex, we have the big university hospitals that are setting the tone for the profession. Patients demand the best and there is a permanent problem of having access to the best. Good money is chasing bad money and local hospitals may be pushed down into an impossible vicious circle.

The basic problem is a managerial one, with a social system governed by egalitarian State regulations and a gradually more and more differentiated model of excellence in the medical technical profession that works only through personal appreciation.

The last impossible problem is that of public health. Because of the enormous weight of the medical profession, public health is the 'parent pauvre' (poor parent) of the French health establishment. It was not taught in the medical schools and may be emerging only now. The State authorities have been unable to develop either their status or their influence. France, therefore, is way behind most of the Western countries on public health. This was made quite clear, for example, with regard to blood contamination that produced a major national scandal.

As a consequence of the traditional elitist system in the hospitals and the lack of influence of public health experts, the French health system spends a much higher share of GNP than most other European countries, with no significant consequence for the health of the population. The French population, for instance, have a very heavy use of psychopharmacological drugs.

The future

In order to face all these problems, the French health system must invest efforts in imagination and money.

The financial burden is becoming unbearable. It tends to weaken the economic strength of the country: almost 25% of GNP goes to social security, which is higher than the total of direct and indirect income taxes. Furthermore, this proportion is growing. Formulas to prevent the spiralling growth have never lasted long enough. There is no regulation that can have an impact on the prescribing doctors. They are general practitioners and patients who do not suffer from the deficit of social security that is paid by the State. How can they be made conscious and responsible? General practitioners are now opposed violently to any control and pressure on their incomes and working habits. They tend to help patients to overcome controls. There are no other regulations available. Hospitals are now somewhat more under control, with the creation of regional accreditation authorities, but they are still the source of growing costs.

What is at stake is the invention of a new kind of regulation that will relieve the State of its impossible responsibility.

In 1945, the legislator had hoped that the regulation could be organized by trade unions and employers' associations, who had quasi monopolies of the management of the social security boards elected by the people. This system provided trade unions with jobs and positions of influence, but did not work as a brake on spending. In the 1980s, the system was more and more crippled by lack of participation and attacks, increasing in the 1990s, by the employers' associations. It is now in a quandary about its future.

The second major working problem area is public health. Some efforts have been made after the blood contamination scandal (see, e.g., Setbon, 1993) but they are only just beginning to have an impact. It is urgent now to begin a general converging effort of training experts to organize practitioners' training and the training of a new research establishment.

The third 'chantier' – frontier of work – should revolve around equality of access. Equality of access is a general value that is accepted in all developed countries, but in France, it has gone so far as to prevent development innovation and adjustment to human progress.

One of the main obstacles to change and innovation is the suspicion of the threat of a two-track medical care system. This is a very strong political weapon used generally by the left to protect any kind of corporatist positions. One should insist very much more on the importance of experimental progress that may help generalize new techniques and drugs. There is a new, interesting fad in networks arrangement that may become very helpful. What is to be blamed is the differentiation that confronts the system in its practices of exclusion.

The French health system should not be presented as a case to admire and reproduce, but it has a specific contribution to offer, which should be encouraged, because its successes, as well as its ailments, are to be found in all health systems. Especially since most health care systems have created their basic features from production-based business logics.

6

Living healthy to an older age – would it be possible for everyone?

Christophe Courbage and Orio Giarini

Introduction

Since the beginning of the seventies, the world demographic tendency shows an increase in the number of people living to an older age. Medical progress and higher standards of living are the main factors that made this evolution possible. According to the WHO (2001), worldwide the proportion of people aged 60 and over is growing faster than any other age group. The world's population grows at an annual rate of 1.7%

People as Care Catalysts: From being patient to becoming healthy. Edited by R. Normann and N. Arvidsson.   © 2006 John Wiley & Sons, Ltd.

and the population over 60 increases by 2.5% per year. In 1990, 18% of people in OECD countries were aged over 60. By 2030, that figure will have risen to over 30%.

As the number of elderly people rises, and as it becomes increasingly likely that individuals will survive into old and very old age, the number of them being affected by a chronic disorder or another illness is growing. What used to be considered a mischance that befell a small proportion of a nation's population is now being viewed as a new standard risk that requires the attention of public bodies, international organizations and others stakeholders. As a matter of fact, one of the main concerns is related generally to the rising health costs resulting from technological advances and the changing demographic structure.

Yet, it is because improvements in health sectors have been increasing, mainly due to technological progress, that the average life expectancy of human populations has risen rapidly. It is because more people are living longer that consumption of health-related products is growing. Besides, older people are not only living longer, they are also living healthier. A growing sector of this part of the population is enjoying a reasonably good level of health. Hence, it is important to view these issues from the proper perspective. We are not ageing as a society, but benefiting from an extended period of good health. The concern is not only the increased spending on health, but also what it is spent on.

Today's health systems are mainly non-funded, pay-as-you-go systems with intergenerational redistribution. Faced with the increases in health costs, they are bound to experience greater and greater difficulties. Private systems and funded systems that allow accumulation of funds early enough to provide for care in later stages are appearing slowly. Such evolution raises many concerns, especially in terms of solidarity and equity. However, as the lifecycle is getting longer, people have the opportunity to be productive for a longer period of time than before, which will, therefore, extend the period of wealth accumulation. This can allow funds or premiums to build up over a long period in order to cover the cost of care in the later stages of life. A good balance of these two complementary systems appears to be the best way to cope with the increase in cost.

In this chapter, we aim to bring together trends, facts, figures, analyses and suggestions to improve our understanding of the health area issues and challenges raised by the so-called 'ageing' society.

Main health-deteriorating causes in elderly people

In general, older people are reporting a greater number of chronic illnesses and disabilities than younger people. This is the case because the body naturally grows older, and older people's physiology is less resistant to disease and less able to combat it. It also comes from the fact that people living to an older age are more sensitive to classic health-deteriorating causes than other parts of the population. These causes are several and we list hereafter the ones that appear to us the most important.

Health statutes of elderly people are influenced strongly by income distribution. Yet, it is not poverty in itself, but rather the degree or scale of inequalities, that leads to the much higher morbidity and mortality figures of those in the lowest income groups. Research (Davey *et al.*, 1998; Kunst and Mackenbach, 1994) has shown that the relationship between income and health is not a direct one, otherwise it could be expected that richer countries, as measured by GNP per head of population, would have better health indicators than poorer ones. This would explain why a country such as Spain has relatively better health indicators than more wealthy countries such as the UK, where income differentials are higher and are increasing. Social inequalities in many forms play an important role in health, mortality and morbidity of populations, and this is accentuated in the older age groups.

Another factor that is also likely to have significant effects on health is changes in the structure of employment, both in past and future decades. The decline in hard manual work and in dangerous, tedious and dirty occupations, which has characterized many modern industrial societies over the past 30 years, may not yet have made itself fully felt in the health status of older age cohorts. Besides, new forms of occupation-related diseases and work-related disabilities, such as stress, sedentary or repetitive strain syndromes, may partly counteract these improvements and have a non-negligible impact on older people.

A third aspect of social life with a strong effect on health and wellbeing amongst older people is that concerned with sociability and loneliness. Surveys (see, for example, Heikkinen *et al.*, 1994) have shown that, in most European countries, there is a positive association between social activity and levels of life satisfaction. While it has been shown that this level of satisfaction was associated negatively with feelings of loneliness. Those in the oldest age cohort are most likely to be confronted with the death of a spouse or friends and social disengagement after leaving work. These events are undeniably contributing to loneliness.

People are living longer and healthier

Old age is not necessarily associated with illness, dependence and a lack of productivity. Nowadays, older people are not only living longer, they are also living healthier. Increasing standards of living have been an important factor in explaining the improved health of older people, whether it is through better nutrition, the practice of sport, giving up smoking, or other reasons.

Technological change, including techniques, medicines, equipment and acts used in health care, has also had a positive impact on the quality of life of seniors. Replacement surgery has helped many people to live a healthier life, and the growing sectors of biotechnology and bioengineering are providing a huge scope for the future. A number of companies are seeking to develop a range of mechanical organs to replace worn-out parts of the human body, such as hip and knee prostheses, heart valves, and, with the technology of cloning, hearts and lungs. Such technologies for making artificial organs are only the beginning. Every part of the human body is now being studied to see how it can be replicated artificially or augmented in some way. For instance, biomedical engineers are developing prototypes of an artificial lung that can be strapped on a belt, or are trying to create a silicon chip that stimulates the visual cortex and may help to restore sight to the blind. There are also various types of substitute cartilage, bone and skin that are working their way through clinical trials. These procedures will definitely continue to extend our active life span.

An increase in health expenditures

Despite the fact that the health care system operates under very different regimes in different countries, its development has shown a similar trend worldwide: a strong growth in expenditure over the last 25 years. It is growing much faster than GDP in almost all countries, and in some it has almost doubled. In most of the OECD countries, health care spending is evaluated at 7–9% of the GDP. The United States is an exception, with nearly 14% of the GDP. In addition, most of this spending is funded through public money. In nearly all European countries, public expenses in health care account for nearly 75% of the total expenditure in health care. This expenditure represents an important part of the public budget as a whole. To spend more resources than are necessary on health care limits the budgetary possibilities of governments to focus on other social objectives that may have a stronger impact on the health level of the population – particularly environmental policy.

The moral hazard issue

One important factor explaining the increase in health care expenses is related to the development of health insurance coverage. In Europe, nearly all the population is covered for health risks. These figures are lower in the United States, where the percentage of people without health insurance was nearly equal to 15% in 1999, yet, they are still substantial.

The extension of health insurance has led to 'agency problems', phenomena well known by economists, especially moral hazard problems. Moral hazard refers to the likely malfeasance of an individual making purchases that are partly or fully paid for by others. Most payments to physicians or hospitals or other caregivers for medical care are made, not by the patient, but by a third party – an insurance company or employer or governmental body. As nobody spends somebody else's money as wisely or as frugally as he spends his own, individuals will overspend, i.e., they will use more services than they would were they paying for the medical care themselves. Hence, the income risk transfer mechanism on which insurance is based is no longer efficient as people increase their consumption of medical care when it is subsidized. Another form of moral hazard also emerges in the risks that individuals choose to take. Well-insured people may be less reluctant to behave preventively than people with a less generous insurance. As individual actions are difficult to observe, insurance companies cannot easily penalize reckless or negligent patients. However, this behaviour has to be put in perspective, as the uncompensated loss of health itself is so consequential. It would be surprising if people smoked because they knew health insurance would cover the cost of their possible lung cancer. One way to discourage such opportunist behaviours is to make people pay a part of their consumption of medical care.

A better way of living

Another important factor explaining growing health care spending is a demographic one. Health spending is more and more positively correlated with age. As mentioned earlier, older people in general are reporting a greater number of chronic conditions and disability. Per capita health care costs are considerably higher than for the working age population or for children (see Spillman and Lubitz, 2000). However, contrary to mainstream opinion, there is a difference between increasing expenditure (which relates to the real increase of value added) and cost inflation. It is important to distinguish clearly between the two different mechanisms influencing health systems. One is health cost inflation, i.e. the same treatment being provided for more money. The other one is the improvement in health services, i.e. a new treatment becoming available that creates additional cost, but at the same time renders superior results. New treatments and advances in medicine and biotechnology are usually costly and will force an increase in expenditure. Yet, they do not only improve our chance of survival, and thus increase life expectancy, but also our way of living. What can be perceived as negative is, of course, that as a consequence, we must face additional expenditures because we have the possibility to live longer and better. Longer life spans mean that health cost will be higher and incurred over a longer period of time.

The 'monetization of the care'

The second factor linked directly to an ageing society, explaining the increase in health expenditure, especially in the sector of long-term care, is what we call the 'monetization' of the care for the elderly. In the past, most of the care for elderly people was provided by the family or by close friends. With the rise of institutional, and especially hospital medicine, and the extension of small families, a shift towards treatment outside the home has taken place. Nowadays, professional caregivers essentially provide this care, funded either through public or private insurance. Those services have always existed; only they were provided for no monetary compensation. Since money was not involved, statistics on health expenditure were not affected. The recent trend to outsource the care for the elderly signifies an attribution of monetary value to the services rendered. This increase in the general expenditure on health does not always change the efficiency of the system nor necessarily increase the welfare of the people. The core case of Denmark and other northern countries shows in any case a good degree of efficiency. Those countries are amongst the ones where dependency coverage is very highly professionalized, with few elderly people living with their children and a significant proportion in residential care or receiving home help.

The contribution of capitalization to providing a better health system

Demographic changes are driving changes in government financing schemes; the proportion of people in work compared with those already retired will decrease, shrinking the tax base as it does. The difficulties of financing the care of more and more elderly people for longer and longer periods of time from an ever shrinking tax base are very great.

Faced with growing health expenditure, changes have taken place in entire health care systems. The main trend in most developed countries is a creeping decentralization combined with a change in funding emphasis from public to a mix of public and private.

The increase in health care cost due to demographic change lies in two issues that have to be distinguished. One is the increase in maintenance to keep a good level of autonomy, whether it is related to mental or physical health. The other one concerns long-term care administered to dependent people. As the risk differs from one situation to another, the coverage system is not necessarily the same.

Yet, whatever the risk, to counter demographic effects and to reflect the commoditization of health services, funding will have to be introduced. The point of the issue is to accumulate premiums over a long period of years so that capital can be accumulated for utilization at an age at which the cost of such premiums would be impossible to sustain. This will allow funds to be accumulated early enough to provide for necessary care in later stages. To what extent could such mechanisms be managed in conjunction with building up pension or retirement funds? Would this imply that for some markets, in respect to certain products and circumstances, we could adopt a common and coordinated approach to life and health insurance? These are the two main questions that should be answered.

Long-term care

In life insurance, the declining mortality trend enables an insurer to guarantee premium rates for the insurance period, i.e. setting the tariff is not problematic. This is not the case for health insurance, where advancing technology and the increasing problem of care dependency in OECD countries have continued driving the costs onto insurance programmes or social security systems. This is a result of the increase in resources needed to care for an ageing population. Covering a 'chronic' risk in a demographically, economically and sanitarily changing environment is not at all an easy task. Effectively, the only way to insure such a risk is to use at least some of the reserve mechanisms, implying contributions or premiums smoothed on part of the lifecycle, whereas provisions are likely to be concentrated at the end of life. As the temporal dimension of the dependency risk is very pronounced, its assessment is problematic.

Dependency occurrence, length of life in a state of disability and life expectancy are particularly difficult to anticipate, making it complicated to tariff dependency insurance products. Moreover, the average future cost of dependency coverage is strongly uncertain and not easily predictable. Hence, as for traditional insurance, uncertainty lies in the gap between individual expenses and the average expense; for long-term care insurance, uncertainty lies essentially in the level of future average expenses. That is why private protection available at present is based on a flat benefit, either in the form of a life annuity or a predetermined capital sum. It does not reimburse actual expenses, since it is impossible to predict advances in medical science and what the financial consequences may be.

One idea is to differentiate the concept of care dependency from illness or acute care. Creating a separate social security branch (as has happened in Germany) has the advantage of segregating health care risks. Long-term care insurance based on the concept of a mandatory minimum paid-up period works similarly to whole-life insurance and may provide the adequate solution for long-term care. If claims experience and investment results are calculated correctly, premiums may not increase.

Maintenance care

Diabetes, cirrhosis and other afflictions kill or disable millions of people every year by ravaging their organs over time. The elderly suffer the heaviest toll. Bio-artificial organs – a merger of mechanical parts with cells grown in laboratory culture – offer the greatest hope for spare parts. They reduce premature death, improve quality of life and serve as vital bridges for seniors waiting for natural organ transplants. Yet, as those spare parts are using high technology, their cost and price may be prohibitive.

One solution to lighten pay-as-you-go health systems, and focusing on maintenance care, could be to utilize part of the life pension fund capital as a complement to health insurance to offset 'excess claims'. The second pillar in Switzerland, which is a compulsory but private pension scheme, could serve as a reference as it is based on capitalization. In Switzerland, second pillar funds can be used to finance the purchase of a principal home or to amortize its mortgage. Part of this capital could also be combined with that acquired from health policies to compensate for current predicaments. Such a system raises various points. To what extent would one be obliged to remain with the same insurer for a lifetime? To what extent would accumulated capital also be accepted by another company? Legislation could be passed to avoid fully deregulated competition that could destroy this type of system.

The importance of the four pillar concept

Demographic trends could be seen as positive if only we were able to devise ways of enabling our 'ageing' populations – most of whom these days enjoy good physical and mental health – to make a valid economic and social contribution to the functioning of our economies over the decades to come. Nowadays, four jobs out of five are in service functions. It is becoming widely recognized that such service activities typically require less physical demands and greater mental abilities. It means that, in principle, workers could easily remain productive longer, especially if retirement conditions could be made more flexible and adequate continuing training, among other things, made available. This implies that the problems posed by demographics could perhaps be turned into opportunities if older workers could be kept working later on a flexible basis.

This is the idea of the four pillar concept, which owes its origin to the fact that in most countries the funding of pensions is from resources drawn from three pillars: the first pillar is the compulsory state pension, based on the pay-as-you-go principle; the second pillar is the supplementary occupational pension, normally based on funding; the third pillar is made up of individual savings (personal pensions, personal assets and life insurance). The fourth pillar involves supplementing the first three pillars with resources from a fourth source, that is, income from part-time work for some years after reaching retirement age. Because it helps to lighten the growing burden of funding pensions in the future, the fourth pillar has become one answer at least to the enormous problem of pension financing in the years to come.

This reorganization of the ends of careers and the new age-management strategy it implies – in which gradual retirement is destined to play a key role – also corresponds to many of the changes (in quality of work, lifecycle, etc.) which are specific to our contemporary service economies. Global retirement, often referred to as partial or part-time retirement, offers a transitional period between full-time employment and full retirement. The worker, instead of working full-time one day and fully retiring the next, can reduce work hours according to graduated and agreed schedules, while drawing part-time pay (and in some cases some form of State subsidy or partial pension). The right question to examine is that of the management of a work force of relatively mature years, usually better qualified and who, up until now, has been discriminated against on the basis of its age. Working longer is possible if working conditions in firms are modified – gradual retirement, flexible work schedules, continuing training, and so on.

There are a number of advantages for employers and workers alike. For the employer, gradual retirement reduces the wage-cost of hours worked, raises productivity per hour, reduces absenteeism, increases job satisfaction, makes for better age management and frees older workers for training duties, among other things. For the employee, it makes it possible to adapt work to his/her changing abilities, reduces stress and increases job satisfaction, gives him/her the opportunity to benefit from continued membership of a work team and from inclusion in the work place and provides him/her with free time to develop extra-occupational activities. By being productive longer, elderly people would stay integrated longer in society, a fundamental promoter of social cohesion and a factor known as primordial to staying in good health, and to limiting future spending in our health systems.

The fourth pillar, then, forms part of the theory that an ageing population, rather than being a problem, can constitute a positive challenge for our firms, communities and individuals.

7

Leadership for health care in the age of learning

Michael Maccoby

Introduction

The troubling issues surrounding health care in the US include: rising costs, over 40 million people without health insurance, variability in diagnosis and treatment and avoidable mistakes that cause harm to patients. Solving these problems is proving extremely difficult, not only because the Government does not provide universal health insurance, but also because solutions to quality problems conflict with incentives and values in the medical profession. Previous work has led us to the view that these issues are symptoms of a medical mode of production that is increasingly maladapted to the explosion of knowledge and the changing economy. The danger for the future of medicine is that this

People as Care Catalysts: From being patient to becoming healthy. Edited by
R. Normann and N. Arvidsson. © 2006 John Wiley & Sons, Ltd.

craft mode of production will be replaced by a manufacturing mode of production that makes the physician into a kind of factory worker. Is there an alternative mode, which addresses variability and cost while maintaining the physician's autonomy? We have studied a very few health care organizations that are attempting to develop a new model. The process of change in these organizations is directed by exceptional leaders. Here, we describe the leadership competencies required and the tools leaders can employ to facilitate change and address resistance. We believe these examples of organization and leadership can be useful to others who are attempting to improve the delivery of health care in America. They may also prove relevant for other countries.

The purpose of our research

The purpose of the study that underlies this chapter was to understand the leadership visions and implementation strategies of not-for-profit health care organizations and academic health centers considered among the best in the USA by an advisory board of distinguished leaders in the field. Furthermore, we explored the leadership competencies and tools required to transform these organizations to adapt to new economic, technological and social conditions.

A report from the Association of Academic Health Centers (Rubin, 1998) stated that the organizational cultures of the centers need to change in order to adapt to new pressures of competition, cost and complexity. A subsequent report, from the Association of American Medical Colleges (Griner *et al.*, 2000) describes positive changes that have taken place in medical schools and teaching hospitals, but cautions that much remains to be done in the areas of cost control and quality improvement. The report states that: 'a lack of shared vision and shared values among key medical school and teaching hospital stakeholders continues to inhibit change'. The report calls for 'new paradigms' and leadership to further the missions of medical schools and teaching hospitals in the new millennium. Our discussion highlights how leaders can respond to these social factors. It focuses on the need to reduce resistance to change through leadership initiatives that help health care organizations move from the craft paradigm to one of learning.

The model of change

We begin our discussion with two basic assumptions. The first assumption is that to improve organizations, they must be understood as social systems made up of people with their own values and purposes. To change a social system, it is not sufficient to install new technology and processes. Leaders must understand how to motivate people to achieve the organization's mission. The second assumption is that, in an ideal health care system, physicians should be able to be productive and creative and to develop trusting relationships with their patients. Without this freedom, the most qualified young people will go into professions other than medicine, where they can better realize their potential. Our early research included in-depth interviews with physician-leaders in order to understand their shared values or social character. We wanted to learn what kind of a health system they would consider ideal. They reinforced this assumption and expressed strong concern about the deterioration of the physician's professional freedom and ability to develop relations of trust with patients. However, while autonomy for physicians can enhance relationships with their patients, colleagues and even their organizations, the physician-leaders we interviewed believe that autonomy in medical decision making when the answers are known (e.g. Class I guidelines) should be discouraged.

We viewed health care from an anthropological perspective, focusing on its changing mode of production. A mode of production refers not only to the use of tools; it describes a productive system of values, beliefs, rules and relationships that may change over time due to new technology, knowledge and innovations in organization. For example, agriculture was a craft mode of production in 1840, when over 70% of the US workforce tilled the soil using methods that had not changed radically for centuries. Today, about 2% of the workforce produces enough food to feed a much larger US population and to export the surplus abroad. Agriculture today is highly mechanized. Large farms are run by agribusinesses. The mode of production, including work roles and relationships, has been transformed. In the process, the independent craft farmers fought the change as long as they could.

Traditionally, medicine has been a craft, organized like a cottage industry with sole proprietors and small partnerships. A few physicians have been able to combine their practice with academic positions. The craft business model has been based on the physician's reputation and personal relationships with colleagues and patients within a guild-like structure. The ideal leadership model, as with other crafts, is master and apprentices, or an ombudsman who represents the interests of his peers. The physician–patient relationship has depended on the patient's trust of the doctor's expertise and caring attitude. For centuries, the technology has been hand tools – stethoscope, scalpel, needles, etc. – and a limited number of useful medicines. The model of care has been biomedical with a strong dose of positive transference to cement trust and strengthen a placebo effect that aids natural self-healing. This model has been disrupted by the rise of organizational medicine, the influence of government, insurance companies and HMOs, the complexity of technology, including IT, the Internet, new medicines and procedures. Furthermore, patients have become more demanding and less trusting.

Following the example of other industries, some health care organizations have adopted a manufacturing mode of production. Physicians have become employees in a bureaucracy or in 'focused factories' that specialize in a particular type of treatment. The physician becomes a 'provider', or else a manager, who is engaged more in monitoring than mentoring and must ensure business profitability. While this approach may fit comfortably into the bureaucratic organization of hospitals, the physician suffers a severe loss of autonomy in the manufacturing model. Contact with patients is measured and according to the physicians, it is limited. A study in *The New England Journal of Medicine* in February 2001, challenges the view that managed care has substantially reduced the duration of office visits. However, a Harris poll (February 21, 2001 in the *Wall Street Journal*) reports that 61% of Americans believe that managed care has decreased the time doctors spend with patients. In addition, when patients do not have an ongoing relationship with a particular doctor but are sent to different physicians, this undermines the positive transference that facilitates healing. To be sure, there has been useful learning from manufacturing, particularly quality management that can be used to address variability in practice and supply management. The use of statistical process control and the development of informatics show promise for both improving outcomes by constructing clinical pathways and controlling costs. However, within the framework of a manufacturing mode of production, physicians tend to resist any further limitation of their freedom to make medical decisions. Unless they are involved personally in decreasing variability, they may see these efforts as 'cookbook medicine' that does not take into account unique patient needs.

Is there an alternative mode of production for health care? Is there one that addresses variability, improves outcomes and cost, yet allows physicians to be creative and retains the best of the craft tradition? Advanced organizational thinking emerging from complexity theory and the most effective professional service companies provide elements of an alternative. In manufacturing, productivity depends essentially on the manufacturer's processes and practices. In professional services, it depends on both producer and client – on coproduction. The lawyer or accountant's productivity rises when the client keeps good records. This is also the case for health care, most clearly with chronic conditions like diabetes, asthma and congestive heart failure. When patients manage their own conditions, keep their own records and medicate themselves, their health improves and medical costs are lowered. Furthermore, as patients gain easier access to medical information on the Internet, opportunities increase for physician–patient partnering.

For health care organizations to make full use of informatics and quality processes, they must become complex, self-organizing, adaptive systems or, stated more simply, learning organizations within a knowledge-service mode of production. This means that professionals will act to further organizational purposes, not in response to command and control systems, but because they have internalized shared values and operative principles. They will not see any contradiction between their autonomy and the organization's goals. For example, physicians will be convinced that by addressing variability, they will be benefitting their patients as well as the organization.

Such a system also needs to use information technology to aid physician decision making and make the patient's experience free of hassles and responsive to individual needs. Thus, the system requires advanced organizational design, informatics and committed, informed professionals – nurses, administrators and technicians as well as physicians.

Furthermore, the ideal health system will challenge, not only physicians, but all health care professionals to work together to improve the health of a community. This requires an expansion of the care model from a purely biomedical craft focus to a biopsychosocial and epidemiological ecosystem focus. It will call for a different kind of medical education, such as the type being pioneered by the University of Rochester Medical School.

Such a system requires leadership skills different from either the craft or manufacturing mode. I first proposed this typology of modes of production in 1998 at the annual meeting of the Association of Academic Health Centers. It was well received and became the leading chapter in *Creating the Future* (Evans and Rubin, 1999). In 1999, I led a workshop with leaders of academic health centers to determine the gaps between the ideal and current practice, using a gap survey. The major gaps indicated in this survey were the following:

- Patient service as the highest priority was an ideal universally stated but seldom achieved. As we will report, we found this gap at all academic health centers, with the exception of Mayo Clinic that is organized to put the patient first.

- Utilization management shared by all physicians is a gap that reflects the prevailing craft mode of production. There is, in general, significant variability in treating the same presenting problem.

- Information systems supporting physician decision making is a gap now being addressed by all the health centers we studied. However, the approaches vary. The danger for organizations is that new information systems are not aligned with a learning culture. (A notable positive model has been developed at Vanderbilt University Medical Center.)

- Individual performance is evaluated regularly. This again reflects the craft model. In general, physicians do not like to evaluate colleagues. However, we found some department chairs that have instituted evaluation systems based essentially on clinical and research productivity. An example is the Vanderbilt Department of Medicine. Some faculty members object to it, but it appears to result in improved productivity.

- Leaders develop relationships of trust. A number of factors cause the trust gap. As health care leaders pressure their organizations to cut costs and improve performance, mistrust increases. However, as we shall discuss, a large part of the problem has to do with a lack of dialog between leaders and their organizations about the need for change and how best to achieve it. Such a dialog must increase transparency about the flow of money.

- Leaders communicate a vision. People want to know what the organization is trying to become and how they fit into this vision. Given the uncertainty in health care, people, especially the middle managers and chairs, want the leader not only to set a clear course, but to explain the logic underlying it and help them to understand the meaning of change for them. If sacrifice is required, they need to know why this will pay off in the long run.

The process of change within health care from craft to manufacturing to knowledge-service is outlined in Figure 7.1.

What we did

In 1999, colleagues and I made study trips to the University of Rochester Medical Center, Intermountain Health Care, Penn State Geisinger, Aetna US Health Care Southeastern Region, the University of Michigan Medical Center, Shands University of Florida, and the Mayo Clinic, Rochester,

	Craft	Manufacturing	Knowledge-service
Structure / Roles			
Organization	Cottage industry	Bureaucracy Focused factories	Complex self-organizing adaptive system (learning organization)
Role of physician	Sole proprietor Small partnerships	Employee Entrepreneur	System stakeholder Leader
Physicians vis-à-vis patients	Authority	Provider	Partner – teacher
Patients' role	Submissive – trusting	Customer	Coproducer – learner
Business Model			
	Personal relationships Reputation	Price Scale Service	Community needs Prevention Health improvement
Operating Systems			
Technology	Hand tools	Electromechanical Chemical	Information Biogenetic
Quality and cost control	Peer review	Statistical process control Utilization management Outcome measures Clinical pathways	Continuous improvement Shared responsibility
Learning	Individual	Organizational	Community
Model of Care			
	Biomedical	Biomedical	Biopsychosocial Epidemiological
Physician Skills			
	Clinical	Managerial	Business Partnering
Style			
Leadership model	Master – apprentice Mentoring Ombudsman	Manager Monitoring	Visionary Dialog Motivating
Values			
	Caring Personal trust Expertise	Profitability Service	Teamwork Innovation

Figure 7.1 The transformation of health care (from craft to manufacturing and then knowledge-service).

Minnesota. In 2000, study trips were made to Scripps Health, the Mayo Clinic, Scottsdale, Arizona, Vanderbilt University Medical Center and Kaiser Permanente in Oakland, California. In November 2000, we facilitated a two-day workshop in Salt Lake City with leadership teams from Mayo

Clinic Scottsdale (MCS) and Intermountain Health Care (IHC). The purpose was to bring together an organization representing the best in patient focused service (MCS) with an organization at the forefront of evidence-based medicine (IHC), to facilitate learning from each other. The results that we will discuss later were enlightening about both the possibilities and limits of inter-organizational learning.

Findings from the study

The findings will be organized as follows:

- the culture of health care organizations and social character of physicians in relation to change;

- the role of leadership, including different types of leadership required;

- the tools available to leaders;

- organizational learning.

Culture and social character

Based on social character interviews and surveys of senior physicians and graduating doctors, we found a dominant shared social character. Most doctors fit a type we termed *expert-helper*. The dominant value for the expert is mastery, including the need for achievement. The expert's sense of self-esteem and employment security is achieved by gaining status and professional respect. Experts find pleasure at work in their craftsmanship and recognition by their peers and superiors. They have a strong need for autonomy. At their best, experts stand for high standards of service and scientifically proven knowledge. They value professionalism, a term with roots in the Calvinist concept of professing a calling to serve. However, at their worst, their obsessive qualities make experts inflexible know-it-alls. They are rooted in a system of master and apprentice, where knowledge is based on experience, at a time when knowledge is quickly out of date and competence depends on continual learning. Thus, the expert's character can be a major roadblock to change. Experts want control over their functions and they resist the empowerment of others, which they see as loss of control. This has been the complaint we heard repeatedly from nurses and some administrators. Physician-experts tend to see their organizations as service functions and do not appreciate the added value of an organization over what they do as individuals. Physicians, like other experts, relate best with mentors, peers or younger high-potential apprentices who share their values.

Approach to service

As defined by Webster's *New International Dictionary*, an expert is 'an experienced person . . . one who has a special skill or knowledge in a particular subject, as a science or art.' Expert comes from the Latin 'expertus', meaning tried, experienced. The expert's awards and diplomas are typically displayed to attest to experience and testify to achievement. The physician-experts we interviewed see the meaning of their work, not only in the excellence of their performance, but also in helping people. Notably, some of the most innovative physician-leaders we interviewed had a somewhat different social character, with a focus on creating a great organization. These leaders were typically productive narcissists, the type described by Sigmund Freud as not impressed by the status quo but 'especially suited to act as a support for others, to take on the role of leaders, and to give a fresh stimulus to cultural development or damage the established state of affairs' (Maccoby, 2003) While the craft-like experts see health care organizations as little more than a support for their craftwork, innovative leaders understand that effective organizations are essential to achieve the goal of better health care in a cost-effective manner. This difference in thinking about the organization can cause a profound disconnection between leader and physicians.

The role of culture

It is also the case that physicians are selected and trained to be autonomous craftsmen. There is little teaching about interdependence or the importance of organization. Physicians are not trained to look at work from the viewpoint of nurses, pharmacists and technicians. The image of the independent decision maker which may have made the field attractive to them is reinforced by their education. The physician-expert is comfortable within a craft mode of production. His ideal organization is his own craft shop, or possibly a partnership. With some frustration, he can also fit into the semi-feudal academic health center. In this organization, the vice president for the medical center takes the role of feudal lord and the chairs become the barons who determine which of their physician vassals are most favored. To carry the analogy further, the academic faculties of specialists are often viewed by the local MDs or primary care physicians as superior beings who demand tribute and referrals but show little or no respect to the peasant-like LMDs. Many of the faculty members we interviewed seek to maintain their autonomy through research grants that allow them to set up their own shops.

These people can justify being part of an academic organization for the prestige it provides them as professors. Because independence, prestige and promotions depend on research grants and publications, service to patients is not their first priority. We also found a culture clash between physicians and hospital administrations. In a sense, this is a conflict between a craft logic of individual authority, self-generated revenue, personal style of care and being the patient's advocate, as opposed to the bureaucratic logic of centralized administration, financial controls, standardized procedures and rules based on principles of fairness. This clash can, at least partly, be resolved by developing a transparent learning culture.

The typical pattern of leading academic health centers results in a corrosive hierarchy of status. The full-time clinicians feel slighted and they also believe that many medical researchers do not spend enough time with patients to maintain their competence. We heard the view that individuals could no longer sustain the triple threat ideal of teaching, research and practice; this could only be done by the faculty as a whole. However, there was not total agreement about this, and some physicians appeared to succeed at combining the three functions.

An exception to the prevailing pattern is the group practice culture, most notably as developed by the Mayo Clinic. At Mayo, in both Rochester, Minnesota and Scottsdale, Arizona, the patient comes first; research and teaching are important, but secondary. Research is aimed at clinical utility. Furthermore, specialists cooperate across disciplines in a way seldom seen in other academic health centers, where patients with medical problems that cross disciplines also lack the benefit of the coordinating Mayo physicians. Mayo doctors are salaried. All departments are treated as cost centers. Physicians can take as much time with patients as they consider necessary. Administrators at Mayo see their role as serving doctors, rather than struggling with them about costs. There is a smaller trust gap at Mayo than in any of the other academic health centers we studied.

The natural question that we asked ourselves is whether the Mayo Clinic and other group practices built on the Mayo model attract physicians with a different, more cooperative social character or, alternatively, whether the different cultures and incentives shape the values of physicians. Mayo favors hiring physicians who have been socialized in the culture as medical students and residents. Since we have not done a longitudinal study of physicians starting with their choice of a place to work, or even a choice of residencies, our answer to the question remains somewhat speculative. However, we were able to interview over 120 physicians and administrators from Penn State Medical Center in Hershey, Pennsylvania and the Geisinger Clinic, which was modeled after Mayo, at a time when the two organizations were trying unsuccessfully to merge. In the clash of cultures, we also observed a difference in the values that were reinforced by the two cultures. We had been asked by the leadership of the Penn State–Geisinger partnership to help develop a common culture based to a large extent on the learning model. In the workshops we held with physicians from the two cultures, there was strong support for this model. On the gap questionnaires, both physicians and administrators indicated the importance of the elements of the model. However, the leadership groups, including some chairs of the two organizations, saw themselves and their counterparts in different ways that emphasized their own virtues and the others' defects.

The Penn State chairs described themselves as open to new ideas, faculty participants in decision making who were able to question authority. They saw themselves as entrepreneurial capitalists. They described the Geisinger physicians as employees of a centralized, bureaucratic collective: rule-driven conformists who did not question authority. The Geisinger chairs saw themselves as placing the highest value on patient service, in contrast to the Penn State faculty who put their publications before their patients. They stated that since they received a fixed salary, financial incentives did not distort their clinical practice. They could take as much time as needed with each patient. They contrasted their cooperative interdependence with their characterization of Penn State faculty as individualistic and careerist. They affirmed their respect for LMDs and the primary–tertiary care relationship and accused the Penn State faculty of being arrogant, controlling and self-serving. These stereotypes distorted the chairs' views of each other. For example, the Penn State faculty was convinced that their clinical care was better than that of Geisinger. That may have been true for some specialties. However, they were unaware that, for example, the

Geisinger CABG results were better than theirs and achieved at a lower cost.

How different were the physicians in these two cultures? If you moved any of them from one culture to another, would their behavior change? In our view, some chairs strongly expressed the cultural values of their organizations, while others were less polarized. After this meeting, we held a discussion with the Departments of Medicine of both groups. The stereotypes were discussed, and the participants agreed to try and create a common culture, using the model of a learning organization. The younger physicians were most clearly in favor of close cooperation and shared leadership. The older ones agreed to make a sincere attempt. They recognized that this required strong leadership to resolve conflict and affirm the common vision. The attempt to create a common culture was short circuited when top leadership could not work together, and the board of directors voted to dissolve the merger.

The role of leadership

Think of the workplace roles in health care in terms of a three-dimensional space. On the X-axis are the pure service roles, measured according to their competence or market value. At the low end are the custodial staff, security workers and so on. On the Y-axis are the pure knowledge workers, including laboratory staff and researchers. Between these axes is the knowledge-service sector that could be termed *solutions work*. These are the people who apply knowledge to produce service, ranging from lower-level transactional roles, such as scheduling and payments, to the professional roles of nurses, administrators and physicians. From a market perspective, the most valuable of these roles is the leadership that must integrate all the roles and inspire people toward a common purpose. In the future, more of the transactional roles, and even some of the professional functions, will be automated by the knowledge workers. It will become easier for patients to schedule appointments, pay bills, examine test results and even question diagnoses using the Internet. Some of the physician's administrative, and even clinical, tasks for chronic conditions will be automated. The role of physicians may change as outcomes become more similar and care becomes more regularized by guidelines. Then, competition among physicians will be based less on outcomes and more on either interactional qualities (service) or innovation (knowledge). However, the need for leaders will remain.

We should distinguish between management and leadership. Management is a function, including planning, budgeting, scheduling, measuring, etc. A manager, a professional or a team that shares these functions can perform it. But leadership will remain a human relationship between leaders and followers. Particularly when change is demanded, leadership requires high levels of trust based on the belief that the leader has the knowledge and understanding necessary to adapt the organization to its environment. Health care organizations need leaders at all levels of the organization, and change requires a critical mass of leaders. However, there are two kinds of leader: strategic and operational. Strategic leaders are needed to develop a systemic vision, communicate it and determine a strategy for implementation. Operational leaders are needed for implementation in all parts of the organization. Let's consider the qualities required in both kinds of leader and their relationship.

There is general agreement that strategic leaders need to define a vision, develop an implementation strategy and motivate people to achieve the vision. However, it is not so clear what kind of personality, skills and tools are required for the role. A report by The Blue Ridge Academic Health Group emphasizes that leaders need emotional intelligence, story telling ability and mentoring competence (University of Virginia Health System, 2000).

This leadership ideal does not fit with our experience of effective strategic leaders, particularly within a social system, where key members resist change because it conflicts with both their expert values and independent interests. The strategic leader who aspires to transform a health care organization cannot be an ombudsman who represents followers who find change uncomfortable. He or she must be able to motivate people to change with both incentives and meaningful goals that emphasize patient wellbeing as well as physician opportunity. It is up to a strategic leader to develop an holistic vision that combines three types of logic: business, quality and the leadership required to make physicians and other health care professionals into good followers, as well as leaders in their own areas (Maccoby, 2001).

Logics for change

Logic of business

Strategic leaders need to develop an entrepreneurial vision that is responsive to the realities of their markets. This will depend on competition and the mix of services offered. The

Mayo Clinic Scottsdale (MCS) had to change a money-losing strategy from an integrated delivery system to the traditional Mayo specialties. Kaiser Permanente in Northern California has a large prepaid membership and, therefore, incentives to educate patients and prevent the need for medical visits. These incentives are not present in a system that depends on episodic treatment. To create this kind of incentive for education, a health care organization needs to partner with a payer, such as a large company, which can benefit by investing in the health of employees to gain improved productivity and less costly hospital stays for patients with chronic conditions. This kind of partnership is developing between IHC and the Becton–Dickinson Corporation, and between the University of Michigan Medical Center and the Ford Motor Company.

The logic of business includes efficiency and cost control as well as effectiveness. It includes partnering relationships with providers, payers, patients and the business ecosystem in which the organization operates, in order to both improve the value propositions of the organization and the health of the community.

Logic of quality

Both effectiveness and efficiency in health care depend on leadership understanding the logic of quality, including patient access to care and decreasing variability in diagnosis, treatment and utilization of supplies. Quality includes the aims for improvement emphasized by the Institute of Medicine's Quality of Health Care in America Project. All indicated preventive, acute and chronic care services should be delivered accurately and correctly and at the right time. Services that are not helpful to the patient should be avoided. Safety hazards and errors that harm patients and employees should be, as far as possible, eliminated. A quality system places patient service as the highest priority but also develops the processes that drive out unnecessary costs and minimize patient errors. Developing a quality system, such as that we saw at IHC, requires the informatics to track and measure, as well as operational leadership to engage physicians in developing pathways that make sense to them. But this is not enough. The culture must be that of a learning organization. It needs to institute ongoing research into what works best, as is being done at Kaiser Permanente in California. As long as the craft mode prevails, quality initiatives will be, at best, only partially successful. As Brent James, MD of IHC put it, 'the caring craftsman is increasing the chance of harmful mistakes, because he resists standardizing processes'. However, leaders should recognize that quality approaches could turn into a kind of religious sect. In one large industry, a global survey found over 40 different quality approaches, and the leaders of each one believed they had discovered the true faith. Furthermore, quality experts may establish overly complex guidelines and pathways. At IHC, a leadership team of physician, nurse and administrator simplified the pathways and gained full support from the cardiovascular department.

Logic of leadership

Strategic leaders need to communicate a meaningful and inspiring vision and engage physicians and other professionals in a dialog about its meaning and implementation. This should be a vision of a learning organization with a clear purpose of quality care and the continual development, implementation and transmission of useful knowledge. We find that, for many of the best physicians, it is essential for leaders to explain how changes will benefit patients and the health of the community. These doctors are critical of leaders whose motives appear mainly economic. However, when finances are not transparent, there will be no trust. Leadership of professionals should be neither dictatorial on the one hand, nor consensual on the other. The leader needs to be like a doctor who diagnoses the organizational problem, prescribes a course of treatment and motivates the patient to follow it, even if it requires a change in lifestyle.

In some academic health centers, as in many companies, a mission and value statement resulted from an off-site brainstorming process. The outcome of these meetings typically emphasized values like service to patients, respect and integrity. But these values can become ideals that are used to support the craft value of autonomy. When teamwork is added as a value, this is seldom, if ever, reflected in the reward system. Values are important if they determine the behavior that supports an organization's mission. However, they need to be aligned with the system goals and reinforced by measurements and incentives. To motivate the organization, the leader must conceive of it as a social system. Unlike a mechanical system, in which the parts are designed to serve the system's purposes, or an organic system, in which the parts are genetically determined to serve the system's purposes, the parts of a social system – people – have purposes of their own. Leaders must align these purposes with those of the health care organization.

This also includes gaining support from all the key stakeholders. Boards of directors must be educated fully or they can undermine even the best of visions, as was the case at Scripps Health. University presidents often are not aware of how little board members know about medicine and the issues of health care. Too often, board members adopt the point of view of their personal physician, who may be at odds with the leadership. Strong unions of nurses and technical workers either hurt or contribute to change. David Lawrence, MD of Kaiser Permanente, developed a partnership with unions that supports the transformation to a learning organization. He has also emphasized the education of his board.

Strategic and operational leadership

Change requires both strategic and operational leadership. The strategic leader develops the vision, including value propositions and unique market positioning. He or she determines the skills required to realize the vision and selects operational leaders in administration and departments. Together, they align structures, systems, incentives and partnerships to implement the vision and they lead the dialog with all parts of the organization. Operational leaders determine how the management functions will be carried out in order to achieve operational excellence. They will be coaches who mentor, challenge people and evaluate their work. The operational leader may also build collaboration between teams. The work group has the role of coproduction and innovation. Ideally, members participate in management functions and, as good team members, they help each other to succeed. When there is a good partnership between strategic and operational leaders, an organization develops a shared vision and interactive implementation. This relationship breaks down when a strategic leader gets lost in abstractions and grandiose visioning or when the operational leaders get bogged down in obsessive details.

Of course, there are also chief executives who fail to fill the strategic role and leave their organizations unsure about the direction. It would be ideal if both strategic and operational leaders demonstrated emotional intelligence and showed empathy and caring concern for employees. While this type of intelligence can be essential for operational leaders who need to facilitate teamwork, it is often lacking in effective strategic leaders who have what we are terming *strategic intelligence.* This includes foresight, systems thinking, visioning, motivating and partnering. In some organizations we studied, especially Mayo Clinic Rochester, IHC, Vanderbilt and the University of Rochester, nurses play key roles as operational leaders. In general, an indication of a learning organization is teamwork between physicians, administrators and nurses. Where nurses are empowered, the results can be seen in improved treatment. Nurses, more than physicians, learn to see health care as a system and their values emphasize teamwork more than autonomy. At LDS hospital, a part of IHC, nurses prevailed on surgeons to standardize their procedures, because variability led them to make mistakes. Also, nurses are encouraged to remind doctors to prescribe beta-blockers for cardiac patients. The ideal relationships between strategic and operational leaders have resulted in the shared vision and interactive implementation essential for a learning organization. This ideal relationship becomes unglued when either leader strays from it. We met strategic leaders who became lost in their grandiose abstractions of research greatness at the expense of the clinical enterprise. And we met operational leaders who became lost in obsessive details at the expense of flexibility and focus on the health center's vision.

Leadership tools

A strategic leader has four kinds of tools that can be used to facilitate change. These are:

1. *Budgeting.* Departments should be asked to develop mission-based budgets that are sound from a business point of view and also include efforts to control variability of ordering supplies and to develop cost-effective clinical processes. Investment in IT should be justified according to business logic.

2. *Incentives for managers based on meeting key economic and utilization targets.* This requires building useful measurement systems.

3. *Structuring authority, responsibility and accountability.* Making sure key roles are filled by people with the necessary skills and shared values.

4. *Education.* Leaders typically communicate plans and results, but one-way communication is not enough to

educate physicians so that they accept and internalize operating principles.

One of the best examples of a strategic vision for an academic health center that moves toward a learning organization is at Vanderbilt University. Harry Jacobson, MD, the strategic leader, is using all four tools, but some of the chairs resist accepting the logic of quality. They expressed different objections to us, such as 'cookbook medicine' and 'too economically focused'. It is our experience that lectures, or other forms of one-way communication, will not persuade physicians such as these. They must be engaged in a dialog, which brings out their reasoning. In this process, leaders will either modify plans to incorporate legitimate concerns or explain why not. Dialog brings out the nature of resistance. If it is an expression of the craft tradition, this calls for different leadership action than if there is merely a lack of understanding. If the resistance is not rational and positive incentives are inadequate, resistors should be isolated or replaced. The dialog, properly led, will make it clear to everyone why this must be done. Authoritative leadership will be seen as fully rational and necessary, and the more timid supporters will feel it is less risky to support leadership.

We propose a methodology for such a dialog, using a gap survey based on the elements of a learning organization. Physician-leaders at IHC have used this method effectively to address the gaps that emerged from our study. By using the gap survey and presenting the data in terms of the distribution of responses, rather than as numerical means, everyone can see differences in views and these can be explored to come to a common understanding. This method helps to avoid the situation that often occurs at open meetings, when one angry individual dominates discussion and those who disagree remain silent. We found that physicians tend to avoid open conflict with each other. Processes like the gap survey dialog transform conflict into exercises to understand and resolve problems, or to aid leaders in educating professionals with strong views.

Learning from other organizations

Can health care organizations learn from each other, or is each organizational culture too unique to adopt practices, however effective, from another? In the words of Roger Bulger, MD, speaking of academic health centers, 'when you've seen one, you've seen one.' Does this mean that health care organizations must develop their own solutions to common problems like variability? The answer, we believe, is that organizations can learn from each other as long as they do not try to copy each other. Effective organizations are social systems with a particular purpose or purposes. Learning must fit into this system. It cannot be grafted onto it.

We saw this clearly in a workshop on physician leadership we organized for leaders of IHC and MCS. These organizations appeared to have complementary competencies. IHC is a leader in evidence-based medicine (EBM). Mayo was interested in learning how IHC leadership went about this. Some of the IHC physicians had asked us how they could create more of a Mayo group practice: a patient-focused, cross-disciplinary culture. We thought that by bringing leaders of the two organizations together, they might learn from each other. The CEOs of both organizations agreed this could be very useful. And the chief medical officer of IHC hosted the meeting in Salt Lake City from November 30–December 1, 2000. What emerged from this encounter between two of the best health care organizations in the world is that while both are moving to the learning mode, they are doing so in different ways. They can learn from each other, but neither can graft elements of the other onto its own culture.

IHC and MCS are different social systems. First of all, while both have the purpose of excellent patient care, other purposes are different. IHC is a large integrated delivery system with a health plan. To maintain its huge market share and not-for-profit status, it must demonstrate a commitment to 'the best clinical practice' at 'the lowest appropriate cost.' MCS is part of a unique academic health center in which research and teaching support Dr W. J. Mayo's principle that 'the best interest of the patient is the only interest to be considered.'

Compared to IHC, MCS is a medical boutique for episodic treatment. (Mayo Clinic, Rochester is part of an integrated health care system with geographically dispersed clinics and a health plan.) Another way of looking at this is that the Mayo Clinic derives its tax-exempt 501c3 status based on returning to society the benefits of its education and research. IHC's 501c3 status is based on willingness to serve patients without regard to their ability to pay. IHC's hospital charges are 15% lower than the national average. On an acuity-adjusted basis, the charges at the University of Utah hospital are about 40% higher than charges at LDS hospital, both in Salt

Lake City. While the MCS hospital does provide charity care when it involves a unique service not available elsewhere in their area, their charges are among the highest in the Phoenix area.

The consequences of this difference in mission are that at IHC, there is a conflict between the health plans and physicians whose compensation, unlike that of Mayo, is incentivized according to productivity measures. There are other cultural differences. At IHC, while the conflict between physicians and administrators is related to the mission, there is also a historical factor. IHC leadership came from the bureaucratic hospital system, while Mayo leadership has always belonged to physicians, starting with the Mayo brothers who modified the craft mode to develop a form of cooperative individualism. At Mayo, administrators serve physicians; at IHC, the roles are more equal; however, there is tension about who is in charge. Non-medical leaders at IHC have championed EBM and cost-effective clinical excellence. Mayo has a great tradition of peer review and remarkable openness of physicians to mutual criticism, as long as it is the interest of the patient. However, there has been resistance to EBM. Mayo physicians point out that they often deal with complex health problems that require cooperation across disciplines and do not fit standardized pathways. Although some Mayo chairs have begun to address variability, to do more would require conviction that EBM is both sound scientifically and fully benefits patients.

Both IHC and Mayo left the workshop with a clearer understanding of how they needed to move toward their own ideals. As Michael O'Sullivan, MD, chair of the MCS board of governors commented, 'the value was in seeing how leadership in both of our organizations achieves the alignment of the total workforce toward meeting those aspirations. It seems to me that although the goals may be different, that should not prevent us from learning from one another the essentials of leadership, the need to continue to cultivate leadership that is so important to achieving our respective missions'. IHC is continuing the dialog between leaders and physicians, to increase understanding of their mission and to respond to legitimate concerns. MCS is planning to develop a leadership dialog and to design a version of EBM that fits its culture and values. In doing so, it can learn from the Vanderbilt model, as well as IHC, and develop its own learning program. This is what has been happening.

Conclusions

- There is a strong affirmation from leaders of some of the nation's best health care organizations of the need to move to the learning mode of production. There are elements of the learning mode emerging in some of these organizations.

- There is resistance to change, particularly from physicians whose social character and training support the craft mode of production. Unless the education of physicians focuses on developing the values and competencies for a learning organization, resistance will continue to impede positive change.

- Change requires a partnership between strategic and operational leaders with complementary qualities. Strategic leaders must integrate the logics of business, quality and interactive leadership. They need to use the tools of budgeting, incentives, structuring, education and leadership dialog. Operational leaders must implement the vision interactively, develop teams and maintain the processes and systems. Leaders are needed throughout health care organizations, and without a critical mass, even the most competent and charismatic leader will not succeed.

- Health care organizations are cultures or social systems that have missions or purposes and are composed of people who must be motivated to achieve these purposes. These cultures are different according to their social, political and business environments and traditions, as well as their missions. They select and socialize different values in their key members. Social systems can learn and develop only when leaders align innovations with other elements of the system. Otherwise, new ideas and approaches will be distorted or rejected totally. The good news is that some of the leaders of not-for-profit health care organizations are becoming aware of what is required to transform their cultures and they are providing models that others can learn from, but not copy.

- Policy makers need to understand that solving the problems of health care delivery is not just a matter of adopting new techniques, but rather of transforming a craft mode of production in a way that incorporates the best craft values in more productive, interactive learning organizations. This means that leaders should be selected, not because they are distinguished experts, but because they have strategic intelligence and understand the logics of business, quality and leadership. They must also have the informed support of their boards, which recognize that positive change will provoke resistance.

8

Overall conclusions this far

Niklas Arvidsson

S O FAR THIS BOOK HAS ANALYSED AND DRAWN CONCLUSIONS on important aspects of health care systems based on experiences and illustrations from many countries and systems. Since our next task is to take all this knowledge and propose how an ideal system for health care could look, we will reiterate briefly the main conclusions from previous chapters that we want to bring with us into the next chapter.

Central conclusions from previous discussions are:

- There must be a fundamental shift in orientation within the care industry. Health is what matters. This implies several things:

  —preventive care is one important and underutilized mechanism;

People as Care Catalysts: From being patient to becoming healthy. Edited by R. Normann and N. Arvidsson. © 2006 John Wiley & Sons, Ltd.

—patients must be seen as 'whole' individuals;

—patients must be enabled to coproduce their own health in cooperation with physicians and other care professionals;

—care providers of all sorts and care takers, i.e. patients, face a mutual change and learning process that will question many taken-for-granted assumptions on 'who knows best' in specific situations. In many cases, old prestige and vested interests must be set aside.

- New ways to understand and measure 'value', i.e. the main benefits from the health care system, must be developed.

- Equal, fair and open access to health care is not negotiable. It is a human right.

- Monetization of health care is here to stay.

- Labour market regulation, and especially that related to people over 65 who still want to and can work, is an important part of the financing of the health care system. In addition, it is an important part of preventive care.

- Care must become more targeted to patients' needs, both in terms of how it is financed and how it is organized.

- Financing must provide stronger incentives for all concerned in the creation of health, and should stimulate both better health among people and improved internal efficiency within care-providing organizations and their members.

- Ownership is not an important issue in most situations. Alternative forms of organizing and owning care organizations must be encouraged.

- Regulated norms and standards for care must be met by all.

- Care must – in some cases – be unchained from geographical, time-based and professional limitations.

- Care-providing organizations must be enabled to integrate disciplines, technologies and important resources such as the time, effort and will of patients according to the specific needs of the care-providing situation.

- Strategic and operational leadership in care organizations must be reorganized and improved. Missions and visions must be clarified and strengthened in many cases and new organizational practices are definitely needed.

- The rooted professional mission of helping human beings that resides among physicians and nurses must be protected, while at the same time allowing for and stimulating increased internal efficiency within care organizations.

Now we are ready to move into the next chapter, where we will create an idealized design of a health care system that meets the criteria necessary to achieve the conclusions reiterated above. The ambition of the idealized design is to outline the characteristics of an efficient, effective and sustainable health care system.

9

An attempt to create an idealized design

Bert Levin and Richard Normann

E VERY SYSTEM IS A RESULT OF ITS HISTORY. WHAT HAS survived, and even thrived, through history often turns out to be strong, but there are also deficiencies that can be understood only in the light of history. Such blockages may be about organizational compromises or solutions that once were rationally motivated, but which now exist mostly because they once were introduced. Or they may be elements that have survived but are now obsolete because of scientific development, or because of changes in the values and behaviour of people.

We have developed an idealized design that, by definition, is free from such historically conditioned restrictions. This idealized design was developed originally in a multiclient project regarding health care in a southern region of Sweden

People as Care Catalysts: From being patient to becoming healthy. Edited by R. Normann and N. Arvidsson. © 2006 John Wiley & Sons, Ltd.

called Skane, which we headed as consultants. The Skane region is responsible for health care for 1.2 million Swedish citizens living in the region. Thirty-three municipalities in the region are responsible for old-age care. The Swedish government is, of course, also heavily involved in both health and old-age care. Representatives for both the region and the municipalities – politicians, administrators and professionals – were engaged in the project. Other participants in the project included trade unions, companies and organizations in the field of health care. All were heavily involved in the process of the project, which in all covered about a year and a half. One of the outcomes from the project was this idealized design.

The question we have asked ourselves is simply what a model, a logically coherent system for health care and care of elderly people, ideally could look like, starting from the current knowledge level of science – no wishful thinking here! – and known driving forces of change. Thus, in this phase, we disregard totally what the system looks like today. In Sweden, for example, the system is built on cooperation between State, county council/region and municipalities. The idealized design is so general that it is applicable everywhere in the industrialized world, where the thought of solidarity is a basic feature of the health care system. Of course, as current knowledge of science and known driving forces develop over time, old idealized designs become obsolete and should be revised, which means our idealized design is time-bound.

In the process we identified a number of central requirements that have to be fulfilled by the idealized design:

- The model must fulfil the needs, demands and challenges that come from the customers of the system. This applies to both active 'coproducers' and, until now, more passive 'receivers'.

- It must live up to the challenges that are a result of, not least, technological development – what we have called the *opportunity revolution*.

- At the same time, it must fulfil the basic conditions that consist of fairness/solidarity/risk sharing, quality and rationality. These are the constants in an otherwise changing environment.

We further assume that the political system must exert control over how much of the taxpayers' money should be used for health care. Nobody should, in practice, have the right to assign freely the money of the taxpayers. The democratically elected politicians, on *one* occasion, should decide how much should be paid in taxes and how these are to be distributed between different areas – and thus how much of it should go to the health care system. The actors who use more money than they have been attributed should be forced to take the responsibility for exceeding costs and for their losses. They should not be able to squeeze more money out of the political system when it is too late. This is a democratic demand for decency that the system ought to fulfil.

As mentioned, the system must also have the ability to adapt itself to changes in the environment. Big and complex, hierarchical and bureaucratic systems become too rigid and unable to change. The failures of the countries with planned economies are demonstrating this. But purely market-oriented solutions for whole care systems have not proved to be successful either. Most obvious is, of course, that they cannot live up to the demands of fairness and solidarity. The attempts to build market elements into a mainly collectively owned, financed, managed and organized care system have been associated with difficulties, as we have already seen. Often the end-customer has no real power, money, knowledge, alternatives or real choices. The attempts at systems of buy-and-sell easily become affected and artificial so long as the negotiating parties ultimately have the same principles. Contracts by tender have several advantages: they increase competition and push down costs. But if the service that is put up for tender is defined too narrowly, there is a risk of freezing the system in its current form and inhibiting the power of development. The contract may restrict the possibilities of the entrepreneur to try new ways. A well-functioning market today is often about system development, not about buying or selling standardized products and services. The buy–sell model as used today is best adapted to entirely standardized products.

So, neither planned economies nor traditional market alternatives lead to the necessary dynamic processes. A solution for the future health care system needs both political and administrative steering and market functions in such a mix that the system is provided with good self-developing characteristics, a high ability to adapt itself to changes in customer needs and demands, and to new technology and knowledge.

In the crossfire between the opportunity explosion and the manifest and latent needs of the customers we have, as described below, discerned four care logics that reflect basic differences of their tasks. They are defined by the customers'/patients' needs, available technology, level of knowledge, geography, etc. Today, these care logics are mixed up conceptually, organizationally and administratively. Thus, none of them is working very well. In addition, all of them are exposed to strong change. We are convinced that the care of tomorrow should build upon these care logics as points of departure, and that by doing this, greater use and better results can be obtained from any given resources.

Figure 9.1 illustrates some of these fundamental points of departure of the idealized design.

Thus, the idealized design disregards deliberately the administrative organization of today. This means, for example, that we have disregarded intentionally circumstances fundamental to some systems, like distribution of work between the law-making State, region/county council with responsibility for care of the ill and municipalities with responsibility for

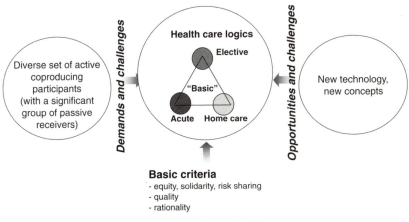

Figure 9.1 Conditions of the health care system.

home nursing and old-age care. The model is developed with a future ten-year perspective and on a high systemic level.

The ambition of the idealized design is not to make authorized institutions implement the model as it is. The model is a foundation for future work. This work should be carried out from a general perspective and with an holistic view, even though reforms of parts of the organization can be implemented gradually, if they point in the direction of the general solution. During such a change process, however, we have no doubt that the idealized design, while being useful as a guiding vision, would not be realized exactly as we have sketched it here. The change process would result in learning that would, without doubt, unveil even better visions.

A logical next step in the process is to identify existing restrictions between the system of today and the idealized design, to see which restrictions can be passed and which are not possible or desirable to pass, and after this to revise the design accordingly. Thus, the revised design turns into an ambitious, but attainable, model for health care and old-age care for the year 2015, a realistic stretch goal, a vision. Starting from this stretch goal, a programme of actions is elaborated with a concrete succession of steps to realize the stretch goal.

Main characteristics of the idealized design

The basic structure of the idealized design is that every customer receives a certain amount (in the form of insurance), the size of which is determined by the political system, and which can be used only to choose to adhere to a 'basic care unit' (BCU). Different basic care units compete for customers and take full responsibility for the health care and the old-age care of their customers. The BCUs can equip themselves with their own care resources, or can buy such services.

Executives responsible for the care logics – which cut across all BCUs – are appointed by the political majority. They certify and approve the quality of the BCUs and of all suppliers of principal services to the BCUs. Care logic responsible executives are not only responsible for certification, but also for system developments taking account of the care logics. They also negotiate different agreements with various suppliers of care, agreements that can be used later by the BCUs to the extent that they like.

We will now describe more thoroughly the idealized design by going through the different main actors of the system and their tasks and roles. Many functions of the design touch many of these main actors. We apologize for the fact that this description contains a certain amount of repetition, but we include this for pedagogical reasons.

The main actors are:

- the individual – as citizen, voter, taxpayer, owner of rights and duties – an ever more demanding customer and a more coproductive patient;

- the political leadership;

- basic care units (BCUs);

- care logic responsible executives (CLRs);

- 'companies'[1] with internal production resources in a certain geographic area, and the municipalities;

- external suppliers of care.

The individual as citizen, customer and patient

The individual as a citizen chooses the political leadership that has the overall responsibility for the system. He pays the taxes of the system that are decided by the politicians. He is entitled to care.

The individual as a customer is supplied with economic resources, the capitation remuneration, decided on by the political leadership. The customer chooses to adhere to one of the competing BCUs, which then receives his capitation remuneration and takes the responsibility for his care. The capitation system can also be described as a means by which the political leadership can budget the activity. The capitation may vary for different citizens considering age and other sociodemographic factors. The customer has the right to choose between available BCUs, and also the right to change unit on certain occasions if he is not satisfied.

---

[1] We use the term 'company' with some hesitation. The mode of incorporation is not important here. Instead, it is the organizations' mode of operation as entities on a competitive arena that matters in the idealized design described in this section.

It is difficult, in advance, to tell how many will use their right to choose actively between different competing BCUs. But we know that many people value their health highly, in other words, that important questions are at stake when choosing BCUs. The customers who do not use their opportunity to choose will be divided between different BCUs. A possible method would be to assign the customer the geographically closest unit. It is still important to acknowledge that the most important effect of the right to choose is that it puts the whole system, i.e. all BCUs and their care suppliers, under pressure. Even if just a few people actively use their right to choose, it forces the whole system to shape up and behave better.

In this model, the customer has the right to choose a BCU, but not to choose freely between different doctors and other resources supplied by the unit. We have also considered a model that would give the customer the right to a free choice of doctors and of other resources, but we dismissed that thought. It is a model that in reality requires an individualized capitation system, where the customer has the right to use freely his remuneration and also takes the responsibility to make sure that the remuneration is enough to cover the care that he needs. But what to do with the customer whose care money is used up too quickly or is not enough to cover upcoming serious and expensive needs? Such a pure individualization of the system of remuneration would miss the whole idea of insurance. With the BCU being responsible for the health of its customer, there is risk compensation, where healthy and ill customers, cheap and expensive customers, counterbalance each other. You gain on the swings what you lose on the roundabouts. And for extreme risks there is a system of reinsurance. But in this case the customer cannot have free right to choose between any doctors. He has the free right to choose a BCU, but this unit then has the responsibility to choose the proceedings that the customer needs. Every BCU is obliged to accept every customer who wants to adhere.

Sensible BCUs that realize that they are in competition with others will, of course, be sensitive to the desires of the customer, but the customer cannot demand to get any treatment, service, care or doctor regardless of costs. Successful BCUs make sure that the customers have, for example, sufficient and possibly quite generous freedom of choice regarding physicians, etc.

The system should aspire to develop its customers into active coproducers instead of being passive receivers. It should be a priority to make it easier for people with small resources to take the step towards becoming active participants in the system.

The political leadership

The task of politicians is to take an overall responsibility for the health system (of a certain geographic area); to make sure that the system develops in a way that is beneficial to the customers, regardless of who owns the production resources that are used. This coincides well with what WHO calls 'stewardship', and which is pointed out as a central task of the politicians who, ultimately, are responsible. It is an overall responsibility to make sure that the system as a whole gives to the citizens what they need. It is not a responsibility, however, to operate directly the production of required services. Neither is it a responsibility that is limited to the use of one's own production resources.

The political interest and the political responsibility are today concentrated on those parts of the health system that the politicians, via taxes, are financing, and on production resources that are publicly owned. However, a health system that is functioning well includes – to an increasing extent – elements of other kinds of financing apart from taxes, and also contributions from production resources not publicly owned. On an overall level, the political leaders must see to it that the whole system – regardless of by whom it is financed or produced – cooperates to the good of the citizens (Figure 9.2).

If the focus of politics has been, and still is, to the left of the matrix, it must also, in the future, be able to engage the very rapidly growing competences and participants that are to be found to the right of the matrix. This has nothing to do with

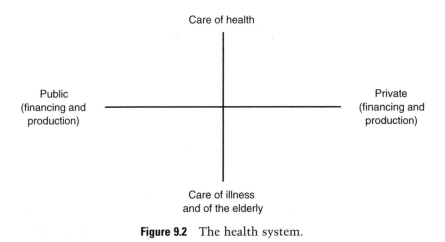

Figure 9.2 The health system.

getting stronger ownership influence, but with finding forms for smooth cooperation.

It is important to remember that the idealized design is about the democratically elected political leadership of the system, regardless of which it is, how it is appointed and organized. Thus, the model does not depend on whether it is a national government, a regional political authority or a municipal authority that has political responsibility of the system – or whether it is a well-functioning cooperation between political institutions on different levels that has this responsibility.

The political leaders also must see to it that the system supplies necessary social services to all its citizens, regardless of their private economic situations. No other authority can guarantee that the solidarity requirement of the system is carried out. In fact there are two questions of distribution in connection with the availability to everybody of health care and old-age care. The fundamental one has to do with unpredictability. Nobody knows beforehand who, during a life span, will be requiring care. There are individuals who, for genetic reasons or due to their lifestyles, belong to the groups of high risk, and others who are running a very small risk. But there is also an important random factor. This question of risk and distribution is close to a pure insurance way of thinking, except that the solidarity way of thinking requires a system that also includes customers at high risk. This has to be taken into account by the idealized design.

The other mechanism of distribution is about how much individuals, with a strong or with a weak private economic situation, should contribute to the system. The idealized design is constructed in such a way that in this respect, regarding the political level of ambition, it is neutral.

In the model, the political leaders decide about taxes and how big a proportion of them should be used for health care and old-age care.

On a *macro level*, the most important decision of priorities is this: how comprehensive should the collective obligations be concerning health care? It is self-evident that this is a political decision. However, other difficult questions of priorities remain: what should be included in the collectively financed responsibility, how is the tax-financed health care to be defined, and what is to be left outside?

The collective obligation can, in principle, be defined according to two models. It can either define what is included in the obligation, or there can be a general formulation of what is included, together with a precise description of what is left outside the collective obligation. Both methods have been used in different parts of the world and neither one of them has proved to be practicable. There are at least two reasons why it is difficult for the political system to define the political obligation. One of them is that the ever-changing knowledge frontier is moving ahead and is changing what it is possible to achieve within the health care area; the daily advancements of science and technology always challenge the borderlines from yesterday. The second reason is that it is very difficult politically to make clear which illnesses or health needs are to fall outside the collective obligation.

Every question has to be handled at a level where sufficient competence and decision power is available. This is why we have come to the conclusion that the political system should define the collective obligation in rather general terms – the definition should, to a certain extent, remain open. After that it is in reality the task of the different professions, in the value-creating meeting with the customer, to decide what the collective obligation should cover in concrete situations and within a given budget frame.

The bulk of the taxes that are to be used in the system are channelled into the system by a so-called *capitation principle*. This means that every citizen is assigned remuneration (in the form of an insurance policy) that he transfers to the BCU of his choice. It remains to be discussed how the capitation system should be designed. But some kind of formula that takes into consideration sociodemographic factors, above all age, seems natural. The alternative with the same amount for all individuals hits too unevenly considering the actual costs of care caused by different groups of people. The other extreme, with an individual examination of each capitation remuneration, becomes bureaucratic, expensive and in violation of integrity.

The task of designing a reasonable capitation system will not be overwhelming. There are experiences and thinking about this in many places around the world. Insurance 'companies' have great knowledge about the kind of risk appreciations that must be made. When designing a capitation system, there must be a combination of risk and insurance thinking on one hand, and political ambitions regarding distribution and the extent of tax financing of the system on the other. This means that the task of designing a capitation model in the end must be the task of the politicians, but they can take advantage of the knowledge of the insurance profession.

One important development resource of the model is the CLRs. They are responsible for the rational development of the system according to the care logics that have been identified. They develop offerings for their respective care logics that are placed at the disposal of the BCU. The CLRs, among other things, have to certify BCUs and suppliers of core services of care to the system. Thus, it would be unsuitable for them to be financed by the BCUs, which are dependent on their certification. Therefore, it is natural for the political leaders both to choose CLRs and to grant money for their financing. This becomes part of the overall responsibility that the political leaders have for the health care system.

Historically, the people politically responsible for the health care system often relied on their own production resources. To a high degree this is the case in Sweden, where the regional county councils are dominating producers of care for the ill, and where municipalities are dominating producers of care for the elderly. The idealized design is neutral concerning the question of ownership of means of production. In this model, production can take place regardless of the owners of the resources, if only the other parts of the model are respected – i.e. collective financing, capitation, the free choice of the customers to choose between different BCUs that may decide how they want to organize their activities, and CLRs as development engines. But today, in fact, the political system owns a majority of the means of production of the health care system. This is a reality. The task of politics should be to exert an active ownership of these production resources. But in the model there is a pure ownership responsibility that has to respect that one's own production should compete on the same terms as other care suppliers, both on the 'home market' and on other markets.

By creating a 'company', based on one's own production resources, and where the political leaders constitute the shareholders' meeting, the ownership responsibility of these resources is taken care of. The shareholders' meeting, in turn, appoints a professional board of directors that has the responsibility to run the activity in a successful way. This 'company' cannot expect any additional contribution of tax money or any special advantages in competition with external suppliers, but has to show its vitality on strictly its own merits.

In our model, politicians have two main tasks: one is to take an overall responsibility for the health care system, where much of the *development responsibility* lies with the CLR. The other is about *financing* – both to be responsible for the implementation of the idea of solidarity by a collective financing of, above all, the capitation remuneration, but also by grant financing of CLRs. An auxiliary third heavy task, which in reality does not follow the model but rather is a historically given reality, is to exert ownership responsibility for one's own production resources. But to make the model function, it is required that the ownership responsibility is taking place in a neutral competition environment and without any advantages to its favour.

The model is designed to give the political leaders a firm grip on the collectively financed costs of the system. In many cases this is not the situation today, when tax-financed health systems are running with huge deficits, which are left to the political leaders to take care of in the end. It is democratically urgent to give the political leaders good possibilities to control totally the tax-financed costs. The citizens elect their politicians. They should decide on tax collection and how the taxes should be distributed between different collectively urgent purposes. When this is done, no sector should be able to make any kind of free ordering of more tax money, or to exert any blackmail on the political leaders.

The big collectively financed item of the idealized design is the capitation system. To this is to be added a limited grant financing of the CLRs and of some staff functions. And that's it! The production resources of the region and of the municipalities are financed by their successes, in competition with other suppliers, on the home market from selling their services to the BCUs and thereby indirectly benefiting from the capitation remunerations and the tax financing of the health care system. These production resources may also be successful on the export market. The BCUs receive their capitation remuneration from the citizens and possible other remuneration from the reinsurance system. No model can be immune to political leaders who want to give way to pressure for more money, but the idealized design is constituted in a way that makes it relatively easy for the political leaders to insist on their original decisions on how much tax money should go to the care system. It facilitates the control of the collectively financed costs by the political leaders. This is a democratic demand of transparency.

Another task, which only the political system can handle, is the work for general health of the people. In our model, the

BCUs will have strong economic incentives to work with preventive care on an individual level. The healthier the customers of a BCU are, the better both for the customers and for the BCU. But the general work with the health of people – environment policy, traffic policy, drug policy, etc. – is a kind of infrastructural input that can only be taken care of by the political system.

The idealized design brings forth one more question of financing upon which the political leaders must decide. As we have described above, the demographic development, the medical–technological opportunity revolution in a wide sense, heavier competition for well-educated personnel and the high evaluation of health, will result in increasing costs to the system. (We believe it might be a question of doubling the health care component of GDP in a ten-year time frame.) There is a dramatic increase in costs in store for us. We are convinced that it will not be possible to finance this cost expansion entirely by increasing taxes or by reprioritizing within the public sector.

How, and on what conditions, should different kinds of complementary financing be allowed? The political leaders must answer these questions. We think the appropriate set-up is a comprehensive collectively financed fundamental system that rather freely can be complemented by the addition of increased private fees, collective insurance, private insurance, employers and other private sources. If you do not allow these types of private financing to complement the tax-financed system, there is a great risk that we get two parallel systems: one that is collectively financed and that gradually will lose quality and support from customers and citizens; another that is privately financed, mainly by insurance, and that provides better services and gradually will win an ever-greater adhesion. We think that such a development would be an unlucky one. It would result in a deficiency in solidarity, it would seem to split the population into different classes and it would also be inefficient and cost driving. The most important thing here is to underline that the idealized design is totally open with regard to whether such complementary financing would be allowed or not. The model works well both with and without the allowance of complementary financing.

Basic care units

The BCUs should be open to all citizens of the region. Every citizen/customer has the right to choose the BCU to which he wants to belong. He also has the right to change to another BCU, according to certain rules, if he is dissatisfied or thinks another unit is better. The BCUs do not have the right to send away any customer who wants to adhere. They have the full responsibility for the health care and old-age care concerning those who have adhered. The customers give their capitation remunerations to the BCU to which they adhere.

The question about a reinsurance system is closely related to the capitation model. We assume that the capitation remuneration would be set according to a fixed pattern. Every BCU has the full responsibility to give necessary care to its customers, i.e. those who have adhered to the BCU in question. To finance this, the BCU has at its disposal the sum of capitation remunerations that these customers bring. By necessity this implies that the costs of the unit, regarding the care of certain customers with very costly needs, will exceed the capitation remunerations of these customers. In return, there will also be customers who contribute capitation remunerations without needing any care at all. There will be both deficits and surpluses on individual bases.

There are good reasons for BCUs to insure themselves against getting a large number of extremely costly customers. This can be done by a so-called reinsurance system. The political leaders should cooperate actively in making such reinsurance systems available to the BCUs. This is part of the responsibility of politicians when building a financing system based on solidarity.

To be allowed to establish itself, each BCU has to be approved and certified by the CLRs. This implies that the BCU agrees to follow certain rules established by the CLR, that there would be controls on certain services and audits of economic management. Reinsurance to cover the costs of extremely care-demanding customers and illnesses and, for example, to build up a certain economic stability, a certain financial solidity, would be imposed on each BCU.

The units compete with each other to make customers adhere to them. In relatively densely populated areas, where it is natural that several units will establish themselves, competition will be sharp. In sparsely populated areas, by necessity there will be fewer units, and the real opportunities to choose will be limited. By experience, we know from other areas where rights of options have been implemented, that everybody will not, or does not care to, make an active choice.

Therefore, mechanisms must be introduced to refer the customers who do not use their right to choose to the different BCUs. However, experience shows us that even if only few people use their right to choose, this influences the whole system strongly, also to the advantage of those who do not exercise their right to choose.

Different BCUs will turn out differently. Certain units will acquire new resources – aurists, physiotherapists, psychologists, children's doctors, etc. Others will have few of their own resources and will prefer to sign agreements that will give them access to resources and competences outside the unit. We believe that all units in reality primarily are geared towards their close geography. However, in bigger cities the units may also concentrate themselves on different customer segments, e.g. on certain language minorities.

The healthier and less care requiring the customers are, the better it is for the BCU. This is a result of the capitation remuneration model. But, as already mentioned, the units have no right to turn away any customer; no matter how bad the prognosis. On the other hand, the remuneration system results in an interest of the BCUs to try to prevent their customers from becoming very care demanding. The model includes an economic incentive for the BCU to push for effective preventive and health-reinforcing activities concerning its customers.

Care logic responsible executives

The concept of the word 'logic' originates in organization theory, where one main principle is that every organization must *reflect the characteristics of its tasks*. Technologies, available knowledge and other contextual factors influence the tasks and how these are connected to create a pattern. The patterns themselves – the care logics – in a certain situation are more or less given. They are defined by real needs, by available technology, the available level of knowledge, fundamental values and the views of mankind – ethics. In the short run, we cannot influence the care logic itself. *However, we can influence how we organize ourselves to reflect the inherent care logics.* In other words, we identify the fundamental logics and in the short term regard them as an independent factor that we cannot influence. At the same time, we regard our own organization and its way of functioning as a dependent factor on which we can have influence.

The most fundamental management task in every activity is the creative identification of the logic of the activity, and after that, the design of the management system, organization, control system, personnel policy, communication, etc. All this should reflect and support the logic of the activity. This is the reason why perhaps the most common problems in an organization have to do with the fact that the new activity logic develops in a way that is inconsistent with the old organization (e.g. because of new technology or new competition or new types of demand).

As we mentioned, our point of departure is to treat care logics on the whole as given. But this is not the case in the long run. During the coming years we will have an accelerated development and changes by leaps in the care logics. This is due to a combination of the IT revolution, medical technical development and communication development, plus the mapping of genes. Therefore, it has never been more important than now – as has been pointed out in many places in this book – to build dynamic, self-developing characteristics into the care system.

We can characterize a number of general care logics as a result of our work to try to understand citizens/customers/patients on the one hand, and when trying to identify technological restrictions and driving forces on the other. On the one hand, there are the needs, demands and wishes of customers. Since we, according to our points of departure, want to regard customers as coproducers and not as passive receivers, the customer side will also provide their own competences, networks and other resources that influence care logics and our possibilities of organizing ourselves accordingly. On the other hand, a number of challenges and opportunities are the results of the technological (in a wide sense) side. Current technology makes it possible to carry out care in a certain way. At one level we are able to discern two types of new opportunity:

1. Emerging new technology that makes it possible to fulfil *existing needs and demands* in a completely new way (compare, e.g., distance care or Losec in relation to earlier forms of therapy).

2. New technology, pharmaceuticals included, which opens up possibilities to fulfil needs and to *do things that today we do not consider possible and do not even define as needs because the technology does not yet exist*. These new possibilities will influence not only the supply side (the way we handle diseases/create health), but also

gradually the demand side (customers will have new wishes and will make new kinds of demands).

Four identified care logics

While working with care logics, gradually four major patterns crystallized. These are the following:

- basic care;

- emergency care;

- elective care;

- home or distance care.

These may be illustrated by the triangle in Figure 9.3. From a customer and patient perspective, these logics can

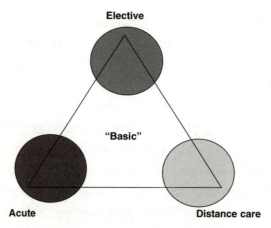

Figure 9.3 Health care logics.

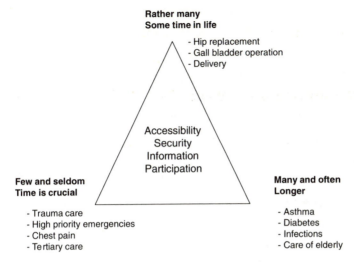

Figure 9.4 Health care logics from a customer and patient perspective.

be summarized in some main dimensions, as shown in Figure 9.4.

According to our diagnosis of today's health care system, different care logics are not only mixed up but also mixed up in a way that tends to disturb and destroy each one of them. Since primary care does not work as expected, customers choose emergency care that is included in the system, and this creates an imbalance leading to a number of vicious circles. The description of care logics that is made here is not necessarily logically watertight, but builds on a pragmatic fusion of a large range of dimensions and viewpoints.

We will indicate some trends and desirable directions of development for the four mentioned care logics that have been identified during the duration of the project. This is a prioritized area of development for two main reasons. The first reason is that many things imply that here is where the large relative weakness of the European health care system lies. The second reason is that the frontline for making customers more like coproducers, instead of passive receivers, is a necessity and unavoidable trend in the future. The main direction here is to centralize and specialize the 'heavy' emergency care.

The development direction of elective care is towards concentration and decentralization. Centres for different kinds of elective care can be allocated to different places. Maybe also different kinds of elective care will be bought from places outside the region, and in the same way, centres of elective care within a region may try to sell their competences to other regions and countries.

We can assume that technological development will continue, and even accelerate, the trend towards replacing what was previously done in care institutions by home nursing, and even – which is included in this care logic – more generally by care 'at a distance' and by using 'mobility' or other decentralized and dispersed 'care delivery systems'. Old-age care belongs to this group, but there is also a growing group of chronic diseases that can be treated at a distance and for which now a number of actors on an international basis are developing specialized systems, e.g. asthma, diabetes, dialysis and high blood pressure.

The system of health care and old-age care ought, gradually, to be organized more clearly according to these four logics. This will not happen by itself. To support a development in this direction there is a need for carefully prepared and systematic inputs. This is particularly intricate since the care logics will inevitably cut across many organizational and ownership boundaries, and will have interdependencies with each other. We are talking about achieving system developments towards these care logics without ownership or line responsibility. To accomplish this we have installed, as a central input of the idealized design, what we call CLR units. Initially, we envision four CLR people appointed by the political leaders: for basic care, home and distance care, elective care and urgency care. Their task is to stimulate different production units to develop offerings in cooperation, suitable for their respective care logic. Together with different care suppliers, they will develop frame agreements or tender agreements, which the BCUs then may use when buying services.

We see the CLR executives as a necessary organizational reform to stimulate the system to develop in line with the care logics, which we have identified as gradually becoming more and more important. We have considered giving CLR units their own resources, thereby ensuring their power in the system, but we have abandoned this solution since it could result in focusing on the use of their production resources instead of on the development of the whole system. We have also abandoned the thought of turning the CLR people into a pure 'think tank'. To make sure that these people both have the correct focus and can exercise power, in the model they do not get their own production resources but are instead equipped with the right to approve – certify – the BCUs and all suppliers of core services to these units.

The CLR unit is financed by special budgets from the political leadership. Every care logic is ascribed its own resources but all four of them must cooperate closely. It is self-evident that CLR people for home nursing should consider independently a certification application request by the suppliers of, for example, old-age care, and also that the BCUs should be evaluated by the CLR people for basic care, and that care suppliers of heart surgery or hip surgery should be evaluated by the appropriate unit for elective care. However, when certifying a supplier that does not only work within one care logic, the units must cooperate.

When examining suppliers of care to be certified, the CLR people first of all must consider a quality of care control. Questions about economic seriousness and stability must also be examined. CLR people should also have a right to expel a supplier who does not live up to his certification.

The tasks of the CLR also include control of the existence of well-functioning competition between different BCUs and different suppliers of care. CLR executives have the obligation to make competition authorities pay attention to tendencies towards monopolizing and other forms of damaging competition restraints. CLRs are agencies appointed by the political leaders; thereby, they have a responsibility to follow up and report to the political system. However, such control-orienting tasks must not hide their primary task, which is creative health delivery system development.

The production resources owned by the system

The politically managed health care systems of Western Europe to a varying extent all have their 'own' production resources for health care and old-age care. Historically, they have not made the distinctions, necessary today, between overall responsibility for the health care system, system development responsibility, financing responsibility and production responsibility. Instead, in a way that has proved unfortunate to the system, they have mixed these different kinds of responsibility and regarded the whole of it as a responsibility for politicians. Therefore, the political leaders have obtained, or secured for themselves, a responsibility that neither they nor anybody else successfully can exert.[2] The historically given reality is that politically run organizations of health care and old-age care in many cases are dominating owners of hospitals and other care units, even if lately we have seen an increase in private contracts by tender in the system.

This ownership responsibility, however, must not be confused with the overall responsibility of a good health care system to the benefit of the citizens. When it comes to developing a good health care system, production resources supplied by the system itself are, in principle, only one of many possible suppliers who have to compete on the same conditions as other suppliers to produce the best quality and solution at a reasonable price. On the other hand, these production resources may be used wherever they may be useful, also outside their own geographic area, as long as this is done on strict business conditions.

It is worth keeping in mind that, in the business world, there are many examples of how production logics have

---

[2] See also chapter 5.

made it difficult for 'companies' to become more customer oriented.

The production units owned by the system are resources that can, and ought to, work together with different care suppliers and competences of the region to develop a strong base of health care. In some geographical areas there is a possibility to construct a competence cluster of high European class. This requires that the own resources, in the first place, get professional management, and then permission to work outside the region. It also requires cooperation between commercial actors and research resources within the different care areas of the region. However, this is a question that is outside the idealized design, although it is touched upon in the last chapter of this book.

It is central to the model that the own production resources offer their services to the BCUs in competition with other suppliers, on the same conditions. No extra favours or advantages can be allowed. The BCUs must have the right to buy their services from any one of the certified suppliers. The CLR people must put the same demands on the production resources owned by their own regional authorities as on those of other suppliers.

To ensure, as well as possible, such competition neutrality, the own production resources should be organized in one or more separate and independent 'companies'. These must be managed on strictly businesslike conditions. They should not be able to receive loss-covering funds or subsidies from the political leaders. They must not get any extra favours from BCUs or from care logic responsible people. They should have the right to offer their services both in their region and on other markets. The 'companies' will be equipped with professional business boards, appointed by the political leadership. It is natural that the 'company' develops retainer agreements together with the CLR people, but of course on businesslike conditions.

Geographical mobility of customers

We need to raise the question about how the health care system should relate to increasing geographical mobility. Our point of departure is that political systems cover a certain geographical area, whereas production resources and people can move – and do so ever more often – across the geographical boundaries of politics.

Starting with the production resources, it is quite clear both that the BCUs can buy their resources wherever they want in the world, and that the production resources of region and the municipalities can offer their services also outside the region. In other words, the idealized design acknowledges that production factors may work freely and independently of geographical borders.

The next question is what happens to the person from one region that needs care outside the region? As long as he is a citizen of one region, he adheres to a BCU that has the full responsibility for his health care and his old-age care. If he gets ill in Boston, the doctor or carer that he sees there will make contact with his BCU to find a solution that both the BCU and the Boston contact can accept.

The BCU, in turn, will evaluate the desires of the client, the American caregiver's quality and costs. This is a self-evident consequence of the responsibility the BCU has concerning its customer, and the economy and reputation of the unit itself.

The third case is about the person who is not from the region, but who, during his stay there, needs care. Normally, this type of customer has someone at home who takes the responsibility for his health. In the region there are a number of competing suppliers of care – both BCUs and others. In this case, an agreement must be made between the care-responsible person at his home and the care supplier in the region. If this turns out to be impossible, municipality and region in principle, like today, have to handle the situation by balancing humanitarian and economic responsibility.

HMOs and the idealized design – a comparison

One model of financing and organization of health care, which has been developed above all in the US, has aroused considerable international interest. We are thinking of the so-called Health Maintenance Organizations, HMOs. They usually, and in short, imply that the employer adheres his employees – and sometimes their families – to an HMO that then takes the responsibility for the health care of its customers. HMOs can use their own resources and competences or buy required medical knowledge from different providers of health care. Here are some resemblances to the BCUs of the idealized design, but there are also some important differences.

The HMO model includes interesting elements but it has, according to our views, a number of decisive weaknesses. The most important of these are the following:

- It does not include all citizens; many of them fall outside.

- The individual rarely has the right to choose between different HMOs; his employer does it for him. The same applies to the right to change HMO.

- The remuneration to the HMO, the capitation, is decided on in negotiations between employer (and sometimes union) and HMO. Thus, the level of ambition of health care is established on this level and not on a political one.

- Nobody has an overall responsibility for the whole health care system; nobody is exercising 'stewardship'.

- The responsibility for system development is hardly established. There is a risk that the result will be a fragmented system.

- It is a system for medical treatment. It does not include old-age care, which seems natural considering the fact that, normally, employers finance the system. Still, this is a weakness.

- HMOs have the right to refuse customers. This is not the case in our design. Instead, a compulsory facultative reinsurance scheme compensates for biases in member populations, while preserving competition.

Summary

The idealized design can be summarized by Figure 9.5.

As citizens, the individuals elect the political leadership that decides on the amount and form of tax resources to be set aside for the capitation remuneration of the citizens. In turn, as customers, they choose to adhere to one of the competing BCUs. Within the limits of their collected capitation remunerations, the BCUs take full responsibility for the health care and old-age care concerning their customers. The BCU can fulfil this responsibility for the health of their customers with the help of their own resources, or by buying competences from other care suppliers.

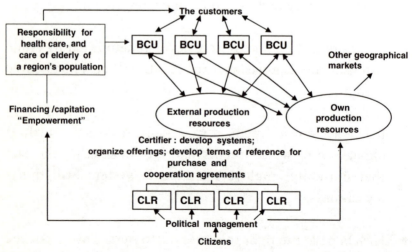

Figure 9.5 Schematic picture of the idealized design.

The political leaders appoint the CLR people and then attribute budget resources to them. The CLRs are responsible for quality control by their certification of BCUs and care suppliers. They also develop modern system solutions that are at the disposal of the BCUs. Many different suppliers and competences can cooperate in such system solutions. They sign retainer agreements for the BCUs.

The production resources that are publicly owned are gathered in different 'companies'. The political leaders have ownership responsibility, but really only a pure ownership responsibility, of these concerns. This implies that they establish requirements of return on investments and of growth, and in the articles of association they decide on the goals of the organization and on main strategic directions. They also appoint professional boards. These 'companies' will work in a strictly businesslike way. They may offer their services to the BCUs, but may also sell their services and competences on other markets, also internationally.

Our ambition has been to develop an idealized design that lives up to the requirements that will be demanded by a modern health care system. The model must be consistent logically. The main requirements that the design attempts to fulfil are listed below. It must:

- give much more power to the customer;

- acknowledge the opportunity revolution, i.e. use the possibilities that the rapidly advancing knowledge frontier opens;

- bear in mind the requirements of solidarity, fairness and risk adjustment;

- have inherent self-developing characteristics, i.e. the ability to change when conditions change;

- guarantee the ability of system development, of new advanced solutions, often in cooperation with different suppliers;

- give the political leaders a chance to exert effective control of the collective financing, and of the tax financing, of the health care system.

We are well aware of the fact that the design is an idealized picture and that reality will demand adjustments. It is neither possible nor desirable to tear down all historically given institutional restrictions that embrace the health care systems of today. However, radically new demands from customers and the environment will oblige rapid and far-reaching changes to take place. We are convinced that these changes ought to take the directions indicated by the idealized design. The risk that any country would move too fast in this terrain is negligible. The threat comes from the slowness of reconsideration exerted by the politicians.

10

An impossible synthesis?

Richard Normann

The uniqueness of health care

Health care is not like any other 'business', for three reasons. One is that it pertains to the value that is of the highest concern to the large majority of people – their health, ultimately the difference between life and death. The second reason is its element of risk and uncertainty: illness strikes unevenly and appears largely haphazardly and for reasons that often escape our comprehension. Thirdly, even though health is highest on the priority list of people, their understanding of it is at the same time thorough and superficial: we know when we are well, but when something goes wrong we have to entrust ourselves to a system based on utterly complex science and technology. Moreover, while many people are much more educated about health today than was the case a

People as Care Catalysts: From being patient to becoming healthy. Edited by R. Normann and N. Arvidsson. © 2006 John Wiley & Sons, Ltd.

couple of generations ago, much of the knowledge that people had acquired has disappeared as we have 'outsourced' the responsibility for our health to public health care systems and the pharmaceutical industry. My grandmother had a much richer diversity of responses to deal with problems than picking up the telephone to call the doctor.

In addition to the above, the notion that everybody has a right to health care has become an integrated part of the belief system that constitutes Western civilization, with its democratic and egalitarian values.

The design of health care systems, therefore, is uniquely complex. The risk factor makes it necessary to have large scale, yet every situation is more or less unique.

In very few fields are the breakthroughs in science and technology as rapid as in the health care area. The pace of change is astounding. *Technologically*, a hospital today is a space-age high-tech environment, and medicines can do wonders compared to what was the case not long ago. The rate of change promised for the future is likely to be even higher, given the advance of science related to genetics, biotechnology and nanotechnology.

Yet, in terms of *management and organization*, health care systems rarely seem to be at the top of the ladder. Admittedly, there are complex and hard to reconcile logics of high technology versus human touch, of politics versus professional values, of focused factory effectiveness versus inherent statistical randomness, of handling both the body and the psyche of people. Still, planning methods, cost calculation techniques and other aspects of organization and administration rarely earn the highest grading. But generally things have improved.

If anything it is in the area of *systemic design* that most health care systems seem not only lagging but outright archaic, whether we refer to the fragmented US system, with its pay-as-you-go cost spiralling mechanism, or the more or less monolithic European systems, which largely use rationing as a technique to protect themselves. The inherent complexities and contradictions of health care that have already been mentioned undoubtedly account for much of this lag. But as Chapter 5 of this book illustrates, the design of the European systems resulted from a great effort of many stakeholders to come together and agree on an overall design, and this design was a deeply imbedded part of the construction of the welfare state. The design not only reflected the state of technology and medical science at the time of its inception, but was also consonant with democratic and egalitarian values, and thus was a key building block in constructing a post-war society.

Building the coalition that could agree on the design also meant building in strong blockages to change. Guild structures, monopolistic privileges and a delicate political balance, as well as a system of rhetoric that can easily mark change proposals as non-democratic, commercial and against the public interest, provide the ground for conservation mechanisms. There is much 'power to block', less 'power to achieve' and 'power to change'. But in the end, the pressures to change will be too much for the old model. Reform or radical transformation is inevitable.

Sadly, a simplistic prescription for health care has been (partial) 'privatization'. The problem is that privatization of defined tasks or units may at best lead to some gains in efficiency, but they do not change the system structure. Other attempts at introducing more dynamism through buyer–seller mechanisms have rarely led to expected results in terms of systemic change and reconfiguration. In many cases such arrangements have become a quasi market, with all parties being part of the same overall structure, with common ownership, as in Sweden, and the constraints to reconfiguration have remained.

What has changed?
Macro-structuring forces

We can summarize the major changes affecting health care systems, and leading to a new 'force field'. The summary builds on four overall driving forces, which all are related systemically and tend to reinforce each other, all pushing up demand for, and cost of, health care. One of these factors – or rather clusters of factors – is the opportunity explosion, led by technology and science, enabling us to do much more than we can afford to do – at least for everybody. The second cluster of driving forces is demographics, which in many ways is the easiest one to discuss, since demographic trends and population 'pyramids' (by age group) can be well established far in advance of their effect. The third group relates to client or patient power, resulting from increased awareness and increased information about individual rights and opportunities. A fourth is the importance of free choice in the modern society. These driving forces will be reiterated summarily below.

It is appropriate here to stress the general transition of society into a new era of value creation, from the industrial era. If the industrial era – which, in turn, took over from the agriculture and craft era – was characterized by standardization, focus on production and large scale, the new era is focused on knowledge, learning and mass-produced individualization. Power is moving from producers to customers. Successful organizations are not so much based on effective factories as on the ability to follow customers, and to organize support for customers' processes of creating value (in this case health) for themselves. The critical competence of today's organizations is no longer production technology but exactly this ability to empathize with customers and organize value-creating activities performed by themselves and by others around the customers (and – of course – harnessing technologies to do this). And the 'offerings' (the organized access to products and services that support the customers' value creation) are no longer typically prefrozen or prepackaged, but are codesigned by the customers in the individual situation. In addition, customers are seen, not as passive and incompetent receivers, but as coproducers of value, possessing existing or potential competencies and skills, which an organization can enable them to use or develop. This shift from an industrial era to an open system value creation era was illustrated briefly in Figure 2.4. The notion of learning, and the 'era of learning', is treated explicitly in Chapter 7 and is also stressed highly in Chapters 4 and 9.

One result of these contextual forces is that there is a new and differentiated risk spectrum that requires differentiated risk management, influencing selectively the behaviour of actors and situations. This is the key theme of Chapter 6. If the risk drivers and the resulting risks are different from what they used to be, and if new actors are important for managing various risks, the financing and incentive system of health care must reflect this.

Secondly, any design of a future system must face a great dilemma: it must continue in the democratic and egalitarian tradition, while recognizing that everything cannot be done for everyone, and that individuals will doubtless have to make choices.

Thirdly, future system designs must be more 'open' in terms of creating more space and stronger incentives and opportunities for further reconfiguration of themselves (for further discussion, see Maturana and Varela, 1987). They must be 'autopoietic' – that is, they must have the capacity for more than continuous improvement and adaptation, namely for continuous reconfiguration and self-creation. The set of stakeholders of the system, and their interrelationships, is therefore an important issue to be resolved. This is the issue of system governance.

Breaking up and reintegrating the system

The new era of value creation that is replacing the craft and industrial eras (without invalidating some of the features of those eras) has led to major restructurings and reconfigura-

tions of 'industries' and 'companies'. Industries have con-
verged and traditional boundaries between them have been
moved or eradicated. Manufacturing industries are becoming
service industries. Banks are becoming financial supermar-
kets – or breaking up into highly specialized niche players.
Software houses have become our 'offices'. And so on.

At the individual company level, a large corporation today
may have broken itself up into a number of functions, each
treated and localized in differentiated manners. The head
office may be in London, the financial holding in Amsterdam,
book-keeping and data processes in New Delhi, call centres
in Scotland, research and development in Silicon Valley, manufacturing in Taiwan and marketing everywhere. Much of its
manufacturing and support services are likely to have been
'outsourced' to other organizations, whether consultants,
manufacturers, data processing organizations or – as is now
happening in the pharmaceutical industry – even specialized
research organizations. The broken up pieces of the old, integrated system, on the other hand, are then integrated in new
patterns through a number of methods such as policies, electronic networks and exchanges, concepts, contractual agreements, planning and budgetary procedures, management
education, culture programmes, and so on. The pattern
follows basic principles of organizations, organisms and
ecological systems: a continuously moving dialectic and more
or less delicate equilibrium between forces of differentiation
and mechanisms for integration. Both are necessary for survival. Structural changes of the kind that were indicated
earlier in summarizing the new force field in health care alter
the conditions of the system and bring about new lines of
demarcation.

Overall guidelines for future designs

All the chapters of this book tell us something about how it might be possible to reconfigure health care systems in terms of new lines of differentiation and necessary integration mechanisms, as well as ideas about where to draw boundaries for the system. I will allow myself to end this chapter by speculating about some of the directions of change that are suggested if we follow the most powerful of these indications. While I draw on all inputs to the book, what follows only engages myself; and while I strongly believe that the speculations that follow have validity, I recognize fully that they are too sketchy to serve as any kind of blueprint. Moreover, the road ahead – even if there is an overriding logic that is common to all health care systems – must always take account of the particular conditions and history of any specific system.

Furthermore, what follows is neither sensational nor new as such. All of it exists already. The macrostructuring driving forces have seen to that. In any system there are always competing inclinations and tendencies. As actors within the system act rationally to defend the existing logic, conservative preservation and continuous improvement strategies always have their proponents. As other actors within the system respond to new macrostructuring forces, alternative solutions and strategies emerge, and they can be found generally either in the internal debate or in embryonic form or as experiments within the system. In addition, as actors outside the system see and seize the opportunities to redefine boundaries or 'invade' systems, we can get good indications of what may happen if defence mechanisms (and I am not saying that such mechanisms should not be considered valid and respectable!) were overcome.

Differentiation lines: care logics

It is a long-accepted truth that health care systems need to reflect both a general practitioner and open 'primary' or 'basic' care logic on the one hand, and more specialized, institutional care on the other. The new technologies, as well as new lifestyle-induced illnesses, make it possible to discern additional distinctions. In a sense, we may think of care logics as leading to an increased break-up of 'the general hospital'. For example, the following are suggested by our studies.

- In *elective care*, highly specialized organizations operating on a more or less global basis are likely to appear.

- For *chronic illnesses* such as diabetes, asthma, hypertension, kidney disease, etc., we see similar tendencies. Such patients tend to have long-term, but to a great extent highly plannable, treatments, which lend themselves to standardized, large-scale solutions, often involving combinations of information and communication technology and specialized medication and technological equipment. Streamlined and focused care organizations with no territorial restrictions are well suited to such activities. They can also use the Internet and other communication technologies to organize local and global 'patient communities', in which patients can learn from each other and develop knowledge that can then be emulated through the system. Focus on enabling technology in such systems will be strong.

- For *emergency care*, systems necessarily have to be local, with the utmost focus on immediate expert access, both physically and with telemedicine solutions, enabling early diagnosis and treatment in ambulances.

- For *basic care*, again the systems must be local, with great focus on accessibility and customer guidance, and with a strong 'enabling' component using telemedicine solutions and rapid, low-cost expert access.

- For *highly specialized care* – advanced cancer treatment, etc. – we will most probably find increased specialization to fewer units serving larger territories.

- *Home care and care of the elderly* will need to function with effective systems for communication, supervision, emergency alarms, self-service testing and support for home-nursing by family members, as well as by specialist personnel.

Integration mechanisms

There are two major foci around which integration must take place: the citizen/customer/patient and the clinical knowledge and practice within the medical profession.

The citizen/customer/patient

Much of what has happened in medicine and health care systems in recent decades – under the influence of industrial thinking and models – has contributed to segmenting the individual – and parts of the individual – from the perspective of the system. Specialized physicians have higher status than general practitioners; hospitals are organized around specialized disciplines; there are few incentives to look at the customer/citizen who is not a patient, but who adopts behaviours that have a high probability of making him one; when people are no longer defined clinically as ill, they disappear from the health care system domain and may not be taken care of, even if they need to be; patient journals and data are typically not easily accessible and neither shared between care units nor with the individual. There are all kinds of good historical reasons for these deficiencies, and a number of sacred cows, as well as professional norms and career systems in the care profession, uphold them, but they can, and need to be, overcome.

Professional clinical knowledge and practice

Medical knowledge as it is used for intervention and care is exceedingly complex. The human body is systemic. Mind and body are inseparable. Having expert medical/technical knowledge is not the same as being good at physical and mental intervention. Actionable knowledge to a great extent is tacit; it can only be learned and emulated by doing and by participant observation. Physical proximity between colleagues within and across disciplines and continuous staging of conversations and rituals are crucial.

The road from the university to the clinical situation is long. The circulation of individuals between different realms of care systems and along the chain of translation of scientific exploration to the clinical situation must be ensured. How can this be resolved? Michael Maccoby, in Chapter 7, addresses many of these questions.

The medical profession, first and foremost, must take the lead in addressing the issues involved here. Professional elites generally must change from within, by staging conversations about basic values and orientations. Physicians may be conservative and protective of their territories and specialist areas, but they also possess pride and norms of excellence that are strong driving forces for change. Physicians need help from system designers to look at career systems and incentive and other reward systems in the profession. Much can be learned from some excellent practices, such as the Mayo Clinic studied by Maccoby, and also from some long-term excellent business companies such as 3M, who have been able to design career and reward systems that simultaneously encourage disciplinary excellence, cross-disciplinary boundary crossings and client empathy and orientation among highly specialized professionals.

Redrawing the boundaries of the health care system

The cover story of *USA Today*, October 24th 2002, deals with the rapidly increasing levels of obesity in the USA (the rate of change obviously proving to be higher than forecast previously), and the ensuing diabetes and other illness problems that 'could break the bank of health care'. In the article, various moves to handle the situation are proposed, but nowhere is the food industry as an actor in the system mentioned. The nutritional habits it has created and continues to promote seem to be taken for granted; the problems are, presumably, to be solved by other actors.

In other countries – such as Sweden – increasing work-life stress resulting from information technology and from the competitive impact of the globalization of business is considered to account for a growing share of health care cost.

Many new and conspicuous drugs address problems, which transcend the borders that have so far generally been seen as illness, and thus the domain of health care systems.

Phenomena such as the above raise questions about where the borderline of health care systems should be drawn. Should health care systems make alliances with the food industry and grocery chains? Should they try actively to move into the internal workings of employers? The Dutch health care system, for one, has increased the risk sharing of employers for health care costs, and care providers like United Health use information technology and health data for what begins to look like assisting employers in their human resources management and operational work procedures.

As we move into the era of open system value (health) creation, in which organizations are 'health creation organizers' rather than only 'producers', we can, in short, expect more initiatives of such boundary crossings. In the new era, organizations will have to take responsibility for the effective cofunctioning of resources over which they have no formal authority.

Financing

The present general financing structure of the European welfare states was invented at a time when:

- people lived shorter lives than today and illness was mainly related to physical injuries related to manual labour efforts;

- people worked during a longer part of their total life span;

- the demographic 'pyramids' were still pyramids, i.e. the ratios between age groups and between the working and the retired part of the population were quite different from today and from what they will be in the foreseeable future;

- the borderline between illness and health seemed more clearly defined;

- the reach of medical science and practice was much lower compared to today's enormous and rapidly growing possibilities, which allow ever more advanced interventions – but often at a very high cost;

- illness was more of a result of non-influenceable (to the individual) 'acts of God' and of social structures, whereas today it is very much a matter of decisions and priorities by relatively much more informed individuals and often 'acts of people'.

In addition, as outlined in Chapters 5 and 6, more people have learnt how to benefit (sometimes manipulatively) from the health care system (the moral hazard issue).

The essence of the changes is that the cost drivers of health care are now:

- more diverse;

- to some extent more diffuse;

- pertaining to a multitude of different actors;

- more a matter of the individuals' behaviour and personal priorities than before.

At the bottom, health care is still a risk management activity, but the risks are more diversified, both with regard to their origin and to the actors who can influence them. This point is very clear from the analysis made in Chapter 6.

A basic principle of risk management is that those who influence the risks should also be incentivized to be accountable, in order to stimulate them towards responsible risk-reducing behaviour. If actors are allowed to 'externalize' the risks resulting from their behaviour (i.e. let others take the negative consequences) the system easily gets out of control with regard to costs.

It is beyond the scope of this book and this chapter to suggest other models for financing health care, but the reasoning above at least suggests a methodology for addressing the issue. Two specific points should be noted:

1. As Chapter 6 demonstrates, increased diversity of the risks and cost drivers should lead to a diversification of solutions – and not only to direct financing but also to changes in work-life habits and regulations, such as their suggested 'fourth pillar'.

2. More priorities about financing will undoubtedly in the end have to be made by individuals. A traditional same-for-all insurance scheme works only under the condition that individuals share values and make priorities within a reasonable, homogenous framework, i.e. that they do not deliberately or irresponsibly externalize their own risks and let others pay for them.

Further discussions of these issues will undoubtedly have to address and reinterpret arguments about democracy and egalitarianism. But unless progress is made, we will risk seeing an increasing sector of health care outside the broad, national schemes, which will have the unintended, but inevitable, consequence of working against egalitarianism. The solution to the dilemma must be to find the demarcation lines between, on the one hand, an equitable system, and on the other, domains where people can make choices about their lifestyle, their work situation and about prioritizing complex risks with important financial implications. If this (difficult) synthesis is not found, we will be rushing into the vicious circle scenario indicated at the beginning of this book.

Governance

The role of governance is, first, to ensure that a system lives up to delivering value to its stakeholders according to criteria of quality, efficiency and ethics. Furthermore, it is to ensure that the system is invested with self-developing and self-regulatory properties, ascertaining long-term innovation and reconfiguration capability.

One might ask whether the current systems sufficiently well reflect the set of relevant stakeholders, as discussed in the previous sections. But this varies between different national systems today.

Part of the governance principle of practically any organization is, or should be, that it be subject to competitive pressures, so that its, structure, functioning and effectiveness are questioned continuously and genuinely. In the proposal for an idealized design of the Skane region, we stress this aspect by allocating practically all money to the citizens, who would then be free to choose between different organizers of systemic health care solutions (many of which would draw on the same production resources but in different patterns). In the end, very few systems not forcing themselves to function in some kind of competitive situation by giving clients power and choice can ensure their survival or their effectiveness over the long term. Giving more information, using more enabling technology and giving financial resources to the citizens, combined with more responsibility for making certain priorities to clients and patients, and ensuring that there always are competing systemic solutions (not the same as privatization, which is another issue) must be high on the priority list for what, in effect, can be regarded as constitutional change. The paradox is that one must often ensure one's own survival by creating more pressure from the outside, if such pressure does not exist or if it is directed from the wrong sources.

11

Positioning our approach

Niklas Arvidsson

I N AN OVERVIEW OF HEALTH CARE REFORMS AROUND THE world, Twaddle (2002) shows that different national systems in the world differ on only a few, but highly critical, dimensions. These include questions as to public or private ownership of health care units. Should the system prioritize general medicine or specialized physicians? Should it focus on preventive care or treatment? How should the system solve its financing? How should it position itself in terms of three important dimensions: effectiveness, equity and efficiency? The main result in this book – the idealized design of a health care system – develops possible and coherent answers to the questions posed by Twaddle. This in itself is a valuable contribution and the main aim and purpose of the book. But we would also like to position our contribution in a conceptual discussion of health care systems.

People as Care Catalysts: From being patient to becoming healthy. Edited by R. Normann and N. Arvidsson. © 2006 John Wiley & Sons, Ltd.

Health Economics is very influential in the case of health care analysis. This line of research has grown quite extensively in the past 35 years, particularly in the USA, and has had impact both in terms of understanding health care systems in terms of economic behaviour and by providing valuable input into health policy and health services research. As the term Health Economics implies, its researchers: '... *often take standard economic theory for granted (like being able to walk or talk) ...*' (Fuchs, 2000, p. 148). Fuchs points out that most health economists come from traditional economics and thus bring with them advantages, as well as disadvantages, when it comes to researching health care systems. The influence of theoretical economics on Health Economics in general is strong (Bridges and Haywood, 2003). Their approach, however, has not entirely been successful in creating effective health care systems for today's societies.

'The systems involved are complex and varied, the forces at work manifold and intricately interrelated, the speed of change alarmingly swift. Patients are concerned and confused; physicians, nurses and other providers are beleaguered and, often, angry; politicians are uncertain and conflicted; managers and health care administrators are stressed and, sometimes, vilified; and investors and financial analysts are seeking to learn whether and how there are profits to be made out of illness.'

Mick and Wyttenbach, 2003, p. 23

Our book aims to acknowledge characteristics of health care systems that traditional health economists have not incorporated in their thinking about health care systems. As has been clarified by Richard Normann in this book and elsewhere, we believe that some of the most important challenges to the health care system are related to developments that benefit from applying an approach not rooted in classical economics. The conceptual foundation behind the reasoning in this book rests on some important, although not exhaustive, characteristics.

Economic systems are not best characterized by emphasizing forces leading to more or less stable states of equilibrium. Instead, we believe that economic systems contain forces leading in different directions and seldom – if ever – toward equilibrium. Prime movers, entrepreneurs, new technologies and knowledge, deregulation or regulation, firms seeking monopolistic competitive positions, governments, capitalists, unions, NGOs and new entrants are just some examples of forces continuously fighting for their interests. In doing so, they also change the status quo. Moreover, we believe this characteristic is an important feature of a future health care system.

Based on the previous note, the system described in the previous chapter is an open and dynamic system, allowing and encouraging learning and change. There must be possibilities for newcomers to enter and incumbents to leave. Incentives for improvement must exist. Moreover, we believe improvement must be defined in relation to a system's historic characteristics, but not necessarily building on them in an evolutionary and additive process. Understanding a system's history is important if we want to understand how it will view the future and conclude which actions to take today, but the conclusion on how the future should look may be the antithesis of today's world view. The inefficiencies of today create reactionary forces, often leading to better efficiency built on new organizational principles tomorrow.

Another important distinction of our model is that resources are heterogeneous and their value differs depending on the objective, approach and the participants present. This means all deployed resources should be acknowledged and valued according to the specific situation and the specific actors when understanding and analysing health care systems. Markets for ownership must exist and work. It is not only governmental capital, but also physicians' and nurses' time and efforts, patients' time, effort and health, use of technology and medicine, and so on, that must be considered and evaluated. Moreover, it is primarily value accrued to customers or patients that matters. As we have argued, much higher emphasis must be given to patients' value than exists today.

Our approach has similarities with the conclusions in a report on the Swedish welfare system (Jönsson *et al.*, 2004). Their report concludes that there are nine major challenges for the Swedish health care system in particular, and international health care systems in general. Their main conclusions, i.e. those that are internationally applicable, are analogous to the ambitions behind this book. They argue that:

- Health care must become regarded as an asset, not an economic burden. The system creates health, which truly is an asset and must become acknowledged as such.

- Productivity and efficiency have deteriorated during recent years and since the possibility to attract new resources are limited in the short run, there is a strong need to reorganize the system, as well as the organizations acting within the system.

- Individual insurance as a payment system is an important way to increase the resources within the system. This should be used primarily for primary care. One possibility the report mentions is mandatory insurance for the entire population.

- Private ownership of health care units should not be restricted legally.

- Criteria for how to prioritize care activities must be official and contestable.

- The health care system and insurance systems for work-related illness are systems that must become coordinated.

- Incentives for cost-efficient use of pharmaceuticals within the health care system must be created and made to influence the system.

- The internationalization process in health care is positive for the system and should be regarded as such.

- Health care must be acknowledged and welcomed as one of the most important growth engines in societies of today.

Thus, based on the points described above, we aim to contribute also to a conceptual discussion of health care systems.

An important issue characterizing our approach is that of power. There are proponents for three different courses when discussing power over decision making (Twaddle, 2002). First, there are those arguing for a fair and just system based on the principle that health is a universal and democratic right for all and access to care must be equitable. This approach is connected closely to a democratic system controlled by politicians. A second approach focuses on the internal organization of the health care system and criticizes the inefficient use of resources in the health care system. Led by a quest for efficiency, this route argues for increased market-based elements in the system, particularly when it comes to decision making over selected care activities for each individual. While the former stance focuses on the outcome from the system and a moral viewpoint, the latter focuses on the operation of the system from an economic viewpoint. A third approach raises the level of analysis by looking at the effectiveness of the health care system, i.e. does it lead to health among the population or not, and how does this approach influence the system? This line of reasoning argues that it is only by introducing the 'revenues' from the system, i.e. health among the people in the system, that the analysis can be complete. When doing so, one is enabled to relate costs to benefits and arrive at a complete understanding of the system. In addition, the hitherto sleeping resources related to work, knowledge and other efforts by health seekers themselves will become unleashed and, therefore, utilized by the system.

Twaddle (2002) concludes the discussion of principles by arguing that: '*Those using rhetoric of efficiency tend to favour market solutions. Those focusing on equity favour democratic control of the system. Those focusing on effectiveness favour professional control of the system*' (Twaddle, 2002, pp. 5–6). This indicates the importance of understanding different stakeholders' own interests and positions when discussing health care systems. As the discussion above indicates, proponents for markets and politicians, as well as physicians as decision makers, are three important viewpoints. But, as this book argues strongly, there is a fourth stakeholder, i.e. those that want to be healthy, that must not be forgotten.

Luckily the fourth group, i.e. those who want to become or stay healthy, is not forgotten. An analysis of the discourse on health care in Holland (Grit and Dolfsma, 2002) shows there are four different discourses in the debate over the health care system. These are, not surprisingly, formed around economics, politics, a medical-professional perspective and a caring perspective. But there is more than discourse on the issue of effects from health care. There is research on economic evaluation of the health care system that includes the health dimension (e.g. Johannesson, 1996; Drummond and McGuire, 2001).

The data being used in evaluations of the health sector focus particularly on costs as share of GDP and Health Accounts, i.e. the share of national accounts related to costs from diseases and bad health in the nation. Improvements in productivity and/or quality in society related to better health among the population are not accounted for (Jönsson *et al.*, 2004). This biased data has, for instance in Sweden, led to a detrimental debate that the health sector only is consuming, i.e. destroying, resources, while the industrial and service sectors produce resources. But this is not the case.

Based on comparing longevity of life and national accounts, Jönsson *et al.* (2004) conclude that the value of improving health is about the same size as the increase in value of the consumption of goods and services in a society. Their conclusions are similar to those reported in a study in the USA (Murphy and Topel, 2003). The main sources to this hidden value lie in the effect good health has on wellbeing in general, as well as productivity and creativity in particular. In addition, the possibility for a good health care system to attract international clients, and thus contribute to exports, is high. This, in turn, leads to a good environment for pharmaceutical companies and other industries, for instance medical equipment, in which they can become internationally competitive and strong engines of national growth. Especially since the demographic situation in the OECD countries indicates the potential future growth of health care.

It is a paradoxical and surprising phenomenon that, in almost all contexts, health care seems to be regarded as a problem and a cost instead of as something that creates positive opportunities. Others have made the same observation:

'Except for Switzerland we now treat the expansion of the health sector as a crisis, instead of as a positive chance to attain prosperity, increased income and work opportunities'.

Eckhard Knappe

The positive effects from health are simply not acknowledged in today's modern societies, and this is detrimental for society at large. It is not possible to evaluate health care without this data and it is not possible to introduce forces creating incentives for improvement and development within the system. As of today, the main decision makers in the system – politicians, physicians, managers and patients – cannot make informed decisions on their actions. The analyses of health care systems have not properly acknowledged revenues, and the discussions of health care in general are one-dimensional. The main question in an alternative approach concerns whether a health care system – including all its dimensions as pharmaceuticals, medical technology, physicians, hospitals, financing, patients' time and trouble, etc. – is effective when relating health effects to overall costs. A central objective with this alternative approach is to alter the decision-making process in a way that the interest of more stakeholders than politicians and physicians receives influential status. Intentionally avoiding the particular intricacies related to methodological challenges in determining the value of health effects, which in itself is a long and challenging detour, our book provides a contribution aimed at meeting the ambition in these approaches.

Appendix A:
A challenge for
economic policy

HEALTH CARE AS AN ACTIVITY HAS IMPLICATIONS beyond its direct impact on the health situation of the individual or of a population. In addition to this, there are reasons to see the care system in the broader perspective of economic policy. Health care is not an isolated phenomenon but a value-creating activity integrated with other value-creating activities, both locally and globally. Care and other activities linked to care create, not only health, but also employment opportunities, and they influence trade and industry, the education system and research and development. This appendix will be about some of the dynamics and potential that another approach to the health sector may help us discover.

People as Care Catalysts: From being patient to becoming healthy. Edited by R. Normann and N. Arvidsson. © 2006 John Wiley & Sons, Ltd.

Cluster-creating factors

According to a traditional view, 'people follow job opportunities'. However, there are people who have reversed the expression saying, instead, that in the knowledge society 'job opportunities follow people'. This is natural if the raw material of knowledge-intensive companies is creative, entrepreneurial people with new ideas. Clusters of knowledge-intensive industries tend to appear where you find this kind of people together with organizations supporting their work. It was, of course, different in an economy based on raw material: the mine could not be allocated where people liked to be, but to where the raw material was found. Now the company is located where the new raw material – knowledge – and conditions for its development are found.

Thus, it is becoming ever more evident that factors like a high standard of living, physical security, culture and also climate are important factors of competition. Furthermore, the knowledge society is characterized by the fact that the knowledge carriers – the people – need to meet not only via the Internet but also face-to-face. Thus, good and efficient communication, above all by air, is another important competition factor.

The first factor, access to raw material – knowledge – has to be provided. Universities and advanced research also helps.

A second factor that is utterly decisive is *the degree of sophistication of the local demand*. Nothing stimulates the development of a company or a domain of activity more than demanding customers with the opportunity to choose. Therefore, the local contact between knowledge workers and a competitive, demanding market is very decisive. It is often from an advanced local system development, together with demanding customers, that superiority arises, which makes a company competitive on international markets.

A third factor that often is mentioned is the importance of tough competition, also locally. Volvo and Scania have developed into two of the world's most successful truck manufacturers, in spite of a very small home market. But to conquer and keep their positions on this market they have been forced into a rough competition between themselves. Similar examples can be found in many regions and industries.

A fourth factor that we have observed often in different contexts is *the manner in which key actors organize and expose their business to subcontractors and other suppliers.* An interesting comparison can be made between, for example, Silicon Valley in California and 'Route 128' outside Boston, which, in its day, was much talked about. The key companies that established themselves and played key roles in each place respectively, had totally different philosophies. The companies of Route 128 had a 'do-it-yourself' philosophy, while their counterparts in what later became Silicon Valley, e.g. Hewlett-Packard, worked totally differently. Instead of doing as much as possible themselves, they encouraged others to become subcontractors and also to present new solutions and suggestions. In this way, in Silicon Valley – as opposed to Route 128 – a great diversity of small companies appeared, some of which later became big and successful.

European health care and old-age care are, in this comparison, much more like Route 128 than Silicon Valley. An interesting effect of this, which may be speculated about, can be observed at Gambro, a very successful company in Lund. In Sweden, they are a company primarily selling products and equipment related to dialysis. Internationally, they are a big service company selling treatment to 50000 to 100000 dialysis patients. This increasing international business is an important reason for, and condition of, the success of the company. However, in principle, it could never have started in Sweden since the care there has been organized in a way that makes this type of service or system development work impossible.[1]

A fifth factor concerns tensions and opposition in general. In an ongoing study (due for publication in late 2005) by Ulf Mannervik and Niklas Arvidsson done for Vinnova, the Swedish Agency for Innovation Systems, we have seen how the conflicts between an institutionalized business environment and creative entrepreneurs with widely different views on how to create business offerings and organize the business system in themselves, became a major factor for strong innovation environments. Seeing the different dynamics in processes leading to an efficient and more integrated business system vis-à-vis those creating a new and different business system, led us to understand the importance of these factors. The innovation environment must be understood in terms of two fundamental processes – one leading to internal efficiency and the other leading to external effectiveness (via a changed business system) and four corresponding dynamics.

---

[1] Gradually some dialysis treatment in southern Sweden has been subcontracted and Gambro has some contracts, but this is a consequence of system development that it has been possible to create on other markets.

Processes and forces supporting each one are constantly happening, albeit with varying intensity and dominance. At the same time, dynamics stimulating each process and/or transformation from efficiency to effectiveness and vice versa grow or diminish organically. All these forces (which will not be discussed in more detail here) must be understood before any policies and actions with the aim of stimulating innovation are decided. This is not the case today.

Our conclusion is that the way in which health care at large will be organized in Europe will be of utterly decisive importance for how the companies in the area can develop advanced business knowledge and international competitiveness, and thus for their international growth opportunities. The starting conditions are good. If health care is allowed to develop in a way that enables the region to become one of the most advanced places for development of products and business ideas in the health care field, the region will benefit from it in different ways:

- The quality of its health care system will be still higher and will continue to develop.

- Therefore, it will be even more attractive to companies to work in the region, and more international companies (or some of their units) will be attracted. This will give the cluster more strength and more job opportunities, and it further enhances the knowledge density, and thus university research and development.

Here, we talk about a virtuous circle in the relations between care, trade and commerce and the region, where all links of the chain reinforce each other – under the condition that the playground is organized correctly.

Two scenarios can be painted also for the development of health-related business in Europe. If, as we said, starting conditions are good, there are also worrying signs. The pharmaceutical industry (which has traditionally been particularly strong in Europe) is now shifting its key research resources to the US at alarming speed. (At the time of writing, the French public authorities have finally discovered and recognized that the exodus is particularly strong from France, where working conditions and negative attitudes are seen as very strong). And our work on both sides of the Atlantic seems to indicate a significantly higher degree of innovation and experimentation in health delivery systems, financing and use of new technology in the US as compared to Europe. Swedish politicians are, for example, debating whether 'profits' within care-providing activities are to become illegal.

If it is correct that 'health' in a broad sense will be a (perhaps *the*) key driver of the economy in the coming era, the stakes are high. Who will benefit depends on what attitudes will prevail and on the overall principles by which the health system (in a broad sense) is designed and managed.

Appendix B: Summary of research on value creation via coproductive meetings

A general definition of 'the value-creating meeting' is:

A meeting where new value is created by combining the resources and competences of all participants in a unique way.

And more specifically with relation to care:

A meeting where health-related value is created by a unique combination of resources and competences of the care system and the needs, values, competences and network of the individual.

To produce a value-creating meeting we need a care system functioning in a coproduction mode. The point of departure

People as Care Catalysts: From being patient to becoming healthy. Edited by R. Normann and N. Arvidsson. © 2006 John Wiley & Sons, Ltd.

of this coproduction is the health of the individual. The meeting is a cooperation between all participants and the care system – e.g. social security, business companies, insurance companies and social service. The participants have demands to be able to cooperate efficiently and have interest in the health of the individuals.

Below is a summary of demands to enable the care system to contribute to value-creating meetings:

- **Flexibility and diversity:**

    —resources to the individual, not the individual to the resources.

- **Individualizing – unique solutions:**

    —the right competence to the right individual, not standardized models based on e.g. diagnosis/age – e.g. individual adaptation of care programmes;

    —an holistic view of the situation of the individual is a guiding rule.

- **Learning and reciprocity:**

    —solutions are developed in cooperation between individuals and personnel;

    —clear systems to correct faults and deficiencies are in place.

- **Transparency:**

  —a distinct meeting place exists that is easy to find and easy to arrive at;

  —clarity over the responsibility accepted by the system (and not accepted by it);

  —clear processes, economy, organization and quality indicators;

  —transparency regarding the functioning of care – an open care system.

- **Support – 'empowerment' of the individual:**

  —the competences and resources of the individual are developed.

- **Autonomous base of action of the individual:**

  —can be economic (e.g. capitation or private payment), informative (e.g. access to individual ways of finding information or 'second opinion') or via rules (e.g. bill of rights).

- **Competences and steering systems to accomplish the points above, for example:**

  —management competences to achieve ongoing development and flexibility;

—the ability to gather resources and to formulate alternatives adapted to the individual and initiate new possibilities;

—competence development of both personnel and the individual as coproducers;

—follow-up of results in connection with the treatment of the individual;

—ownership competences that provide the best conditions for management.

The trend towards diversity

In all kinds of activities it is always a good rule to try to treat every customer or 'case' or 'episode' according to the demands of the situation. Traditionally, in health care, the individuals have been categorized according to their illnesses and, thus, their need for treatment. Many attempts have been made to group together 'patients'. One example of this is represented by a study made by the Swedish Federation of County Councils. It recognizes two main dimensions of the needs of the patients: one has to do with age (older–younger), another with the need for treatment, if it is urgent or chronic. Thus, this classification, like most of them, is based on sociodemographic factors and disease diagnoses.

Many factors today make such models appear too poor and simplified, especially if we want to look at relationships beyond the patient episode. In Figure B.1, examples are given

A more complex view:
The characteristics of the individual

Age	young	old
Education	higher	lower
Information, skill	well-informed	not informed
Network membership	several	few or none
Financial resources	well endowed	lacking
Employment	employed	unemployed
Illness condition	acute/	chronic/
	temporary	handicapped

Figure B.1 Characteristic of individuals in today's societies.

of characteristics that in different ways come out as important to the individual's relation to his health and to health care. In addition to demographic and disease-related factors, we here see that conditions that have to do with resources – both financial and different kinds of knowledge – and competences – like belonging to networks of different kinds – may play a major role. In a deeper study, using advanced measuring methodologies, it would be possible and probably desirable to find some typical, combined profiles of individuals, so-called 'archetypes'. With the help of these, and with a rough quantification of their existence, it would be possible to make an estimation of what kind of contributions, resources and communication you would need to develop and combine to reach the individuals.

The appearance of 'parallel societies'

The development towards diversity implies that people in society, who in one way seem to live together, in an existential sense may, in fact, live in some kind of partly separated 'micro societies', which offer completely different rhythms and conditions. Some examples of such trends towards 'micro societies' that can be discerned are the following:

- *The efficiency society*. This world is characterized by increasing demands and increased productivity. As *citizens*, many young and highly educated people in this 'society' turn their backs on party politics. As *customers in the care system*, especially important to them are high demands on urgent treatments, handling of burnout cases and self-inflicted symptoms.

- *The knowledge society*. Here the *citizens* look for more and more IT democracy. Concerning *care*, people of the knowledge society look for deep knowledge about their situation and demand more. They also require alternative forms of treatment and are clearly candidates for self-care.

- *The lifestyle society*. Here are individuals with a great heterogeneity regarding values and self-expressions. As *citizens*, they accelerate the development of more subcultures and they find their own forms for participation. In *relation to care*, many look at health as a lifestyle, but many are also self-inflicting, e.g. by risky adventure sports. Some look for beauty, others suffer from lifestyle diseases like being overweight.

- *The multicultural society*. More immigrants, among other things, result in this. As *citizens*, here are antagonisms between natives and immigrants, estrangement of immigrants, access to an internationally oriented workforce and EU influences, and there are likely to be more immigrant workers in the future. In *relation to care*, cultural gulfs and language difficulties, but also influences and impulses from other cultures and care systems, can be observed here.

- *The polarized society*. Here are winners and losers side by side, socially and geographically (not least between big cities and countryside). The *citizen* aspect means that unemployed and other groups give up or do not enter and, therefore, are left outside, and geographical boundaries cut, for example, through political parties. *The relation to care* implies that here everybody does not manage to demand, choose and influence, and many neither want to, nor are able to, participate and take responsibility for themselves.

- *The elderly society*. There are more elderly people, and more elderly people becoming older. As *citizens*, this means that more and more people have time to engage themselves in individual actions, but there are also worries about generation gaps and unfairness between generations. In *relation to care*, there is here a growing group consisting of 'older-elderly', more chronic invalids, more multisick elderly, but the main contact with care still takes place during the last 18 months of life.

Clearly observable trends like these prove that traditional segmentation is not applicable, or at least is insufficient to health care. Using the old factors when dividing into groups leads to the exclusion of many individuals, who end up between the chairs. Everyone has to be met on his own conditions. At the same time, fairness implies that health care cannot choose certain 'segments' and push aside others.

Finally, this signifies that concerning health care, you have to understand these general trends *on a macro level* to be able to decide, for example, what type of competences and resources should be developed, and *on a micro level,* you have to learn how to organize every individual's encounter with health care so as to make it value creating.

Appendix C:
Useful abbreviations

BCU   Basic care unit

CLR   Care logic responsible executives

EBM   Evidence-based medicine

GDP   Gross domestic product

HMO   Health Maintenance Organization

IHC   Intermountain Health Care

MCS   Mayo Clinic, Scottsdale

People as Care Catalysts: From being patient to becoming healthy. Edited by
R. Normann and N. Arvidsson. © 2006 John Wiley & Sons, Ltd.

NGO   Non-governmental organization

NHS   National Health Service (UK)

OTC   Over the counter

WHO   World Health Organization

References

Preface

Levin, B. and Normann, R. (2000) *Vårdens Chans*, Ekerlids Förlag.

Normann, R. (2000a) *Service Management: Strategy and leadership in the service business*. Chichester: John Wiley & Sons, Ltd.

Normann, R. (2000b) *Reframing Business – When the Map Changes the Landscape*. Chichester: John Wiley & Sons, Ltd.

Normann, R. and Ramirez, R. (1993) From value chain to value constellation: Designing interactive strategy. *Harvard Business Review*, **71**(4), 65–77.

Normann, R and Ramirez, R. (1994) *Designing Interactive Strategy: From value chain to value constellation*. Chichester: John Wiley & Sons, Ltd.

Chapter 2

Normann, R. (2000) *Reframing Business – When the Map Changes the Landscape*. Chichester: John Wiley & Sons, Ltd.

Chapter 3

Normann, R. (1999) *Läkartidningen*, **46**.

Normann, R. (2000) *Reframing Business – When the Map Changes the Landscape*. Chichester: John Wiley & Sons, Ltd.

Toffler, A. (1980) *The Third Wave*. New York: Collins.

Chapter 4

Normann, R. (2000a) *Service Management: Strategy and leadership in the service business*. Chichester: John Wiley & Sons, Ltd.

Normann, R. (2000b) *Reframing Business – When the Map Changes the Landscape*. Chichester: John Wiley & Sons, Ltd.

Normann, R. and Ramirez, R. (1993) From value chain to value constellation: Designing interactive strategy. *Harvard Business Review*, **71**(4), 65–77.

Chapter 5

Setbon, M. (1993) *Pouvoirs contre SIDA*. Paris: Le Seuil.

Chapter 6

Davey, S.D., Dorling, D. and Shaw, M. (1998) *The widening health gap – what are the solutions?* Townsend Centre for International Poverty Research, Bristol, UK.

Heikkinen, R., Franck, J. and Evans, R.G. (1994) Heterogeneities in Health Status, in *Why Are Some People Healthy and Others Not? The Determinants of Health Populations* (Eds R.G. Evans, M.L. Barer and T.R. Marmor). New York: Aldine de Gruyter.

Kunst, A.E. and Mackenbach, J.P. (1994) The size of mortality differences associated with educational level in nine industrialized countries. *American Journal of Public Health*, **84**, 932–937.

Spillman, B.C. and Lubitz, J. (2000) The effect of longevity on spending for acute and long-term care. *New England Journal of Medicine*, **342**, 1409–1415.

WHO (2001) *Health and Ageing: A Discussion Paper.*

Chapter 7

Evans, C.H. and Rubin, E.R. (Eds) (1999) *Creating the Future*, Association of Academic Health Centers.

Griner, P., Heinig, S., Jones, R.F., Levin, R., Moy, E., Nonnemaker, K.L. and Valente, E. (2000) *Managing Change, 2000*. Washington, DC: Association of American Medical Colleges.

Maccoby, M. (2001) Successful Leaders Employ Strategic Intelligence. *Research Technology Management*, **44**(3), 58–59.

Maccoby, M. (2003) *The Productive Narcissist, the Promise and the Peril of Visionary Leadership*. New York: Broadway.

Rubin, E.R. (Ed.) (1998) *Mission Management: A New Synthesis* (Volume 1). Washington, DC: Association of Academic Health Centers.

University of Virginia Health System (2000) *In Pursuit of Greater Value: Stronger Leadership in and by Academic Health Centers.*

Chapter 10

Maturana, H.R. and Varela, F.J. (1987) *The Tree of Knowledge: The biological roots of human understanding*. Boston: New Science Library.

Chapter 11

Bridges, J.F.P. and Haywood, P. (2003) Theory versus Empiricism in Health Economics – An Analysis of the Past 20 Years. *European Journal of Health Economics*, **4**, 90–95.

Drummond, M. and McGuire, A. (Eds) (2001) *Economic Evaluation in Health Care – Merging Theory with Practice*. Oxford: Oxford University Press.

Fuchs, J. (2000) The Future of Health Economics. *Journal of Health Economics*, **19**, 141–157.

Grit, K. and Dolfsma, W. (2002) The Dynamics of the Dutch Health Care System – A Discourse Analysis. *Review of Social Economy*, **60**(3), 377–401.

Johannesson, M. (1996) *Theory and Methods of Economic Evaluation of Health Care*. Dordrecht: Kluwer Academic Publishers.

Jönsson, B., Arvidsson, G., Levin, L.-Å. and Rehnberg, C. (2004) *Hälsa, Vård och Tillväxt – Välfärdspolitiska Rådets Rapport 2004*. Stockholm: SNS Förlag.

Mick, S.S. and Wyttenbach, M.E. (2003) *Advances in Health Care Organization Theory*. San Francisco: Jossey-Bass Wiley.

Murphy, K.M. and Topel, R.H. (Eds) (2003) *Measuring the Gains from Medical Research: An Economic Approach*. Chicago: The University of Chicago Press.

Twaddle, A.C. (Ed.) (2002) *Health Care Reform Around the World*. Westport, Connecticut: Auburn House.

Index

Index compiled by Liz Granger